Evictions in the UK

Evictions in the UK examines the relationships between tenants, landlords, housing providers and government agencies and the tensions and conflicts that characterise these relations. The book shows how power dynamics are being reconfigured in the post-welfare context of the first quarter of the 21st century, as evictions for rent arrears are becoming one of the most significant threats to both the wellbeing of the social housing sector and the welfare of its tenants.

Embracing both practical and critical approaches, this book offers a comprehensive understanding of the contradictory and thus controversial issue of evictions. It explores the range of perspectives involved in the practice – landlords carrying out evictions, those agencies providing legal assistance to evictees, as well as academics and institutions charged with researching and regulating the process. Drawing on three case studies relating to evictions across Scotland and England, this book provides a comprehensive look at the punitive consequences of poverty (evictions for rent arrears) and status (evictions under immigration law) that are applicable to social housing systems worldwide. Based on original, primary-source data, this book will be a key resource for academics and students as well as policy makers and practitioners in the fields of housing studies, planning, social welfare, and political sociology.

After almost a decade as Housing Aid Worker at Shelter in Glasgow, **Joe Crawford** made the transition to academia. After working in several academic institutions in the UK he established Erasmus Research, a collective of academics and activists.

Explorations in Housing Studies
Series editors: Ray Forrest
Lingnan University, Hong Kong
Janet Smith
University of Illinois, Chicago
Keith Jacobs
University of Tasmania, Tasmania

Explorations in Housing Studies is a series of high quality, research monographs which aims to extend and deepen both theoretical debate and empirical research in the housing studies field. The series is being introduced at a time when housing, in its various dimensions, is particularly closely intertwined with the impact of demographic change, economic instability, the shaping of life chances and wealth distributions and with the uncertain impacts of environmental and technological change. This series aims to engage with these and related issues from a variety of perspectives and methodologies.

Housing in Post-Growth Society
Japan On the Edge of Transition
Yosuke Hirayama and Misa Izuhara

Neoliberal Housing Policy
An International Perspective
Keith Jacobs

Housing, Neoliberalism and the Archive
Reinterpreting the Rise and Fall of Public Housing
Kathleen Flanagan

Evictions in the UK
Power, Housing, and Politics
Joe Crawford

Evictions in the UK

Power, Housing, and Politics

Joe Crawford

Routledge
Taylor & Francis Group
NEW YORK AND LONDON

First published 2021
by Routledge
52 Vanderbilt Avenue, New York, NY 10017

and by Routledge
2 Park Square, Milton Park, Abingdon, Oxon, OX14 4RN

Routledge is an imprint of the Taylor & Francis Group, an informa business

Library of Congress Cataloging-in-Publication Data
Names: Crawford, Joe (Research assistant in housing) author.
Title: Evictions in the UK : power, housing, and politics / Joe Crawford.
Identifiers: LCCN 2020016430 (print) | LCCN 2020016431 (ebook) | ISBN 9780367419691 (hardback) | ISBN 9780367419684 (paperback) | ISBN 9780367817022 (ebook)
Subjects: LCSH: Housing policy--Great Britain. | Eviction--Great Britain. | Landlord and tenant--Great Britain. | Great Britain--Social policy--21st century.
Classification: LCC HD7333.A3 C753 2020 (print) | LCC HD7333.A3 (ebook) | DDC 333.5/40941--dc23
LC record available at https://lccn.loc.gov/2020016430
LC ebook record available at https://lccn.loc.gov/2020016431

ISBN: 9780367419691 (hbk)
ISBN: 9780367419684 (pbk)
ISBN: 9780367817022 (ebk)

Typeset in Sabon
by MPS Limited, Dehradun

Contents

Tables and Figures

Tables

Figures

Acknowledgments

I would like to thank the following: Margaret Malloch. Brigid Daniels, Bill Munro and Douglas Robertson. Keith Jacobs and Tony Manzi. Alasdair MacPherson. Kim McKee and Sharon Leahy. All the housing professionals, third sector workers, and housing lawyers who took part in my research. My former colleagues at Shelter. South Community Homeless Service Glasgow. Social Marketing Gateway, and the Alan and Nesta Ferguson Charitable Trust.

Preface

The Approach, Structure and Content of the Book

This book takes a relational approach to the subject of eviction, focusing on the interactions between people and the worlds they inhabit, in order to give a more nuanced account of the practices and knowledges that arise from these entanglements. This is mirrored by the very structure of the book itself, which brings together three perspectives:

- **The World of Housing**, taking an 'objectivist' perspective that accounts for the macro-level of the broader political economy that governs housing through the state's legal and regulatory functions;
- **The People of Housing**, accounting for the 'subjectivist' perspectives of housing professionals as well as third sector workers from a range of services across the UK. By taking seriously the views and opinions of a range of professionals it is possible to construct a much more nuanced understanding of evictions while accounting for the tensions and contradictions that arise from professional practices;
- **The Practice of Housing**, taking a theoretical view of the codified conventions and forms of knowledge that emerge from the interactions between housing professionals and the objective worlds in which they are situated.

It is important to make explicit the perspective from which this book is written. Part One of the book sets the context, beginning with an epistemically reflexive account of the researcher's own position within the wider world that makes up the universe of evictions and eviction practices. Taking a rather unorthodox (but arguably useful) approach, Chapter 1 locates the researcher within this social universe of professional practice in relation to evictions, and provides the reader with a number of valuable insights into the particular perspective from which the book is written. This is achieved through a series of personal reflections, the purposes of which, are twofold. First, these reflexions are an attempt to expose the ever-present fact that the book's perspective is firmly located in the researcher's journey from practitioner to academic. Second, it attempts to suspend the scholastic gaze of the academic researcher in order to present the point-of-view of the practitioner, prior to being 'influenced' by the forms of scholastic bias that 'infect' intellectual thought regarding matters of a practical nature. This is also important because it provides context to the book and the practical and theoretical subject matter that unfurls throughout its chapters.

Chapter 2 widens the aperture to include the main areas of the legal and regulatory framework to which housing professionals, in both the social and private housing sectors, are subject. By doing so, it becomes possible to stand back and observe the political processes that have driven the interventions that shape the legal and regulatory landscape that govern evictions. Chapter 3 concludes the first part of the book by widening the lens even further in order to account for the larger political economy within which housing and its governance structures exist at the macro-level. Having given an account of the World of Housing, the book moves from the 'objectivist' perspective, to the 'subjective' experience of that world.

In 'The People of Housing', Part II of the book, three separate case studies are presented as evidence, all of them relating in some way to evictions and eviction practices, and all of them accounting for the subjective experiences of those involved. In Chapter 4, the first study asks the question, 'why do social landlords evict their tenants?' This case study presents the views of a range of housing professionals in the social rented sector, a sample that includes front line housing officers responsible for the collection of rent, rent arrears managers as well as senior professionals and chief housing officers. By taking seriously the views and opinions of housing professionals in the social sector who oversee evictions, a comprehensive picture is formed of a uniquely subjectivist perspective, providing an otherwise elusive 'view from the inside'. Chapter 5 looks at the relationship between housing professionals who have statutory obligations towards their tenants and third sector rights-workers who help tenants through the process of enforcing these obligations. In Chapter 6, the final case study focuses on the tensions that arise from the reluctance of landlords in both the social and private sectors in the UK to evict tenants who do not have the Right to Rent as prescribed by the Immigration Acts of 2014 and 2016.

The interview data in the three case studies is presented in a way that gives housing professionals and third sector workers their own voice, without too much analysis or scholastic interference. This provides clear evidence that the relations between different groups – between landlords and tenants, between housing professionals and third sector organisations, and between landlords and the State's immigration-control institutions – are often fraught with tension and conflict. Understanding the processes through which these contradictions unfold in the relations between groups, is the purpose of the third part of the book.

In Part III, the structure of the book is further developed to forge a comprehensive theory/method nexus that combines both the world of housing and the people who inhabit this world, in order to more fully understand the extent to which this relation produces the collective conventions and shared knowledges that constitute the professional field of housing. Chapter 7 constructs a theoretical model that synthesises contemporary social psychology with sociology. This synthetic approach is one that attempts to account for the process by which people move from their own 'internalised' subjective understanding of the world, to the collective conventions that allow people to both understand these feelings and to communicate them to others 'externally'. It is based on the founding principle that action, rather than being an entirely rational process, originates within the infra-conscious 'gut' feelings that a person immediately has about a situation or thing. This chapter charts the process through which these embodied feelings or 'affects' become the sets of collective conventions that are the very foundations of practice and knowledge within professional fields.

In order to explore and understand these tensions and conflicts more fully, Chapter 8 develops the notion of the parallax of professional practice. The parallax of professional practice is the term used here to denote the differences that arise between practitioner groups due to the fact that, although they are dealing with the same issue (in this case evictions), they often have different priorities which generate different viewpoints. It is through examining perspectival differences within and between professional groups that it becomes possible to capture the dialectical relations between structure and agency, the conscious and the unconscious, position and disposition, from which practices emerge. This conceptual tool is used to dissect, in turn, the three case studies, unearthing the hidden dimensions to which mainstream, liberal and common-sense perspectives are blind. This modality of being, the one that professionals hide from both themselves and others, the reality that is masked, obfuscated and euphemised under the cloak of a 'disinterested exchange', is explored in Chapter 9.

This key facet of professional practice is elucidated through the forensic analysis of a further two short interview examples. The purpose here is twofold. First, the analysis shows that not only are professionals immersed in their 'professional worlds', they are often immersed so completely, that they fail to take account of the possibility that their own view of the world is but a (very) partial one, and second, that a 'critical', rather than an 'instrumental' or 'utilitarian' approach to research is the only way to both expose and then overcome this limited perspective. Having begun the book with a series of 'reflexions' that located the researcher within the world of practice, the penultimate chapter presents as evidence an epistemically reflective account from the 'academic' perspective. This completes the journey, providing an insight into the true extent to which perspectives shift, altering how the social world is perceived and understood. It provides evidence that even the fullest and most carefully collated 'subjective' account (from the inside), without the critical means by which to address its shortcomings, produces an all-too partial view of that world.

Chapter 10, the last, asks the somewhat rhetorical question, 'what are the alternatives to eviction?' The research journey ends as it began almost a decade before in the office of a firebrand councillor who had, for as long as I have, been fighting to make evictions a thing of the past. Completing the circle from its humble beginnings in the reflexive world of the housing activist, this book ends with questions that address the potentialities and opportunities for radical change in what is proving to be a very uncertain future. The story concludes with a wholesale rejection of the idea that we can end the housing crisis (and any other crisis for that matter) through tinkering with policy 'reforms' and economic 'innovations'. Instead, the book concludes with a call for something altogether much more radical. Something that, in keeping with the uncertain times that lie ahead, radically rethinks the entire political economy in such a way that reconfigures the provision of essential services, such as housing, in a way that aligns them with other universal services such as education and health.

Part I

The World of Housing

1 Evictions

Reflections from the Front Line

Exposition

The issue of evictions has always represented a significant social and economic problem in the United Kingdom (UK), the United States (US) and much of Europe, and continues to do so today. Each and every year for the last decade in the UK's social rented housing sector, around 20,000 forced removals have taken place out of around 80,000 eviction actions raised in court. With the role-out of Universal Credit, a benefit reform that sees rents go initially to tenants and not directly to landlords, the fears of vastly increasing arrears across the sector have already been voiced (Wilson, 2019). In fact, a number of representative bodies for social landlords have expressed their alarm at the impact that pilot areas have endured on rent arrears increases, with many housing associations claiming that they face economic difficulties as a direct result of the reform (Preece, 2018). Freedom of Information Act data obtained by *Inside Housing* magazine shows that even at this early stage, Universal Credit recipients are now twice as likely to face eviction for rent arrears as other tenants. It may be too early to tell for sure, but it does seem that evictions for rent arrears are about to become one of the biggest threats to both the wellbeing of the social housing sector, and the welfare of its tenants.

In order to introduce the subject of this book it is first necessary to locate myself within the overall assemblage of perspectives and practices that govern and determine evictions. I will begin the book with an exercise in epistemic reflexivity, but rather than turn the instruments of reason upon myself in an academic sense, I will temporarily 'bracket' or 'suspend' the scholastic gaze in order to capture the world I inhabited before I entered the academic field. Before taking up a reflexive position on *homo academicus* (explored further in Chapter 9), I start at the beginning by accounting for the world view of *homo operator*.

In undertaking such an endeavour, it is important to remain alert to the fact that there are, broadly speaking, three types of 'perspectival bias' that can blur the sociological gaze. The first is represented by the *social origins* of the researcher. This includes notions of class, gender, political or religious beliefs as well as ethnicity and status, largely determined by the location of the researcher within the wider social structure. This is presented in the first section of the book, and will represent the beginning of my own journey from practitioner to academic. The second bias that one has to be alert to, relates to the *position that the researcher occupies*, not in the social structure, but within the microcosm of the academic field (Bourdieu and Wacquant, 1992: 38), which in my own case is the field of housing studies. The third bias concerns itself with *the intellectualist perspective* that can be problematic when the researcher fails to problematize their own relationship to reason. To begin, it is therefore necessary to provide an exposition of the political and social situation that I found myself in when I began my journey as a practitioner and when I made the transition to the world of academia.

'Reports From the Front Line'

The front-line accounts are presented in and through two modalities. The first will be a factual account of my role as a Housing Aid Worker at Shelter in Glasgow and the second will involve fragments of the experience, communicated as a series of 'reflections', anecdotal stories that I would have recounted to an independent researcher, had I been interviewed as a research subject. Firstly, a contextual account of the environment from which this book's central ideas were forged.

The 'front line' is located within the cut and thrust of daily life as a Housing Aid Worker, employed by the charity Shelter in Glasgow; a multifaceted role that involved among other things, preventing evictions, either directly or through advice and advocacy. The organisation Shelter emerged during a period of public outrage following the national screening of the Ken Loach film *Cathy Come Home*. The film, aired on the BBC in November 1966 to an audience of over 12 million, told the story of a young couple with children as they experience a series of harrowing injustices that resulted in homelessness and destitution. The gritty drama blurred the lines between fact and fiction as it told the harrowing story of overcrowded slum housing conditions, unscrupulous landlords, eviction caused by a lack of rights and a lack of state housing provision for the homeless. Shelter was launched in December 1966 and quickly set about campaigning for the introduction of rights that would prevent and alleviate homelessness. As well as being a campaign organisation, fighting for better rights and services for the homeless and badly housed, Shelter set up an advice and advocacy service.

As an organisation, Shelter expanded its remit, developing a number of functions. It began as a campaign group, lobbying for legislation to enshrine tenant's rights in law, and has been an effective pressure group for the improvement of housing ever since. Opening Housing Aid Centres all over the UK Shelter built up a solid reputation for providing expert legal advice in what is an arcane and complex area of law. As well as delivering free legal advice and advocacy to anyone with housing problems, Shelter developed a range of roles to support their overall aims and objectives. These included: policy analyses and policy briefing papers in which staff assess housing and homelessness policy at both national and local level, and provide commentary and recommendations. Shelter also delivers training to a wide range of charities, teaching them the basics and providing education on the legal processes, the statutory obligations of landlords and the rights of tenants and homeless people.

Such is Shelter's reputation for its unmatched expertise in the field that this training is also delivered to housing professionals, an enterprise that brings in an extra source of valuable funding. Shelter staff were also in demand as public speakers at events that ranged from high profile national conferences, to small-group talks and discussions as well as workshops. Its' core activity however is to provide free advice and advocacy services to anyone who has a housing issue or finds themselves without accommodation or under threat of eviction. It does this through a casework system, where the staff take turns to be 'on-call' and to deal with cases as they come 'through the door' to their drop-in surgeries, or by telephone through the helpline service.

Reflections 1

I had just finished my postgraduate studies and really had no idea of what I wanted to do. I saw an advert for a Housing Aid Worker at the housing charity Shelter, bought Himsworth's Scottish Housing Law text-book, and crammed for two weeks solid. Remarkably, I passed the entrance test and survived the interview, but it didn't take them long to find out that I had basically 'blagged' my way in. It was a steep learning curve, made possible by the kind patience of my colleagues, and a very understanding boss. A joint Honours degree in History and Archaeology and a post grad in Russian Language isn't the best preparation for working in a legal setting. It took me a while to fully appreciate the demands of this specialized working environment, with its specific procedures, practices and conventions.

Shelter's principle solicitor, the housing law equivalent of Mark Darcy from Bridget Jones's Diary, (hugely talented, massively understated and charmingly clunky in any social setting), often had to take me aside for a quiet word:

'We will only win our cases with legal arguments', he would remind me. 'We use the law, and when the law proves ineffective as a means of resolving the case, we have to accept defeat. We let the case go. What we don't do, ever, is resort to moral arguments. Asking a housing officer how they "sleep at night" is not how we best serve our client's interests!'

It took a long time of being reminded of this before my resistance dissolved and I was eventually 'indoctrinated' into an exclusively legalistic approach to casework. I suppose I saw the problems relating to homelessness as having more than just a legal dimension. I saw them through a wider, 'political' lens. The lawyers did have a point though. When all was said and done, moral arguments were in fact, a very poor means of resolving our clients' problems. But then again, more than the lawyers would like to admit, so too were the legal remedies.

The attraction of the job lay in the wide variety of tasks that had to be undertaken, from policy work, to training, delivering plenary talks at conferences, and being on call to deal with the day-to-day housing and homelessness issues of the general public. Of great importance is the work that Shelter does preventing homelessness from occurring in the first place. This is a vast and multi-faceted undertaking, which involves a wide range of interventions in a number of situations, and one that requires complex, long term strategic planning. The most significant, and certainly the most dramatic procedure for preventing homelessness from occurring, lies in the ability to stop evictions. The law governing evictions is complex and arcane, an area of legislation that was little understood by housing professionals, almost not at all by private sector landlords.

If you are a landlord and you want to end the tenancy, you have to issue the correct notices, at the correct times, with the prescribed information on them. These notices in themselves do not end the tenancy. In the social rented sector, the landlord will issue a notice of proceedings for recovery of possession. Then they have to seek a decree for eviction in the Court (Sheriff Court in Scotland). The *Housing (Scotland) Act 2010* places a requirement on Sheriffs to satisfy themselves that the decree is the last resort, and that the eviction is 'reasonable', taking all things into consideration. These *pre-action requirements* are in the process of being extended to England and Wales. If the decree is granted the tenant(s) have 40 days to vacate the tenancy. Failure to do so within the timescale will result in Bailiffs in England and Wales and Sheriff Officers in Scotland being instructed to oversee a physical eviction. Leave willingly, or be forcibly removed by the police, most probably arrested and possibly charged with something akin to a public disturbance.

The rights of tenants are arcane because housing law is so different from other forms of legal competence. It is, so to speak, a world in its own right. In the private rented sector, the same logic applies but using a slightly different set of procedures. Depending upon what Act governs the tenancy, the landlord will have a sequence of procedures that must be followed for the process to be deemed lawful and legally competent. Failure to follow these procedures renders the process unlawful and the landlord loses the right to be able to carry out the eviction without committing a criminal offence. As is the case for social landlords the private sector landlord has to go to court, or in Scotland, a First Tier Tribunal, to obtain a decree for eviction.

Reflections 2

Our office was in Finnieston, a full decade before Finnieston became the most hip, trendy and gentrified part of town. Rundown and undesirable it may have been back then, but it was reasonably handy for Glasgow Sheriff Court, a geographical fact that was of the utmost importance. I cycled to work daily from the city's Southside in all weathers, the added benefit of which was it afforded me the ability to stop an eviction that was due to take place with as little as 40 minutes to spare. That is, as little as 40 minutes before the housing team, accompanied by Sheriff officers and sometimes the police, turned up to carry out the eviction. Almost daily, a client (most often a woman) would appear at my drop-in surgery, (often with many children in tow), clutching a letter stating that they were to be forcibly removed from their accommodation.

All too often the eviction was for that day and not unusually, it was within the hour. I had it all down to a fine art. I'd take their details and phone the relevant housing office, informing the housing officer that I'd be recalling the decree and that they would be receiving notice of service of the court papers imminently. Then I'd dash through to the office, and distribute the essential duties. One of my colleagues would phone the Sheriff Clerk's Office at Glasgow Sheriff Court and one would phone the Sheriff Officers forewarning them of my arrival. I'd pull on my cleated cycling shoes and hop on my bike, tear down the Broomielaw, along the banks of the Clyde, over the suspension bridge and up to the steps of the Sheriff Court. Surrendering my bike into the care of the police officers charged with performing sentry duty outside, I'd run the gauntlet of inequality. It was called thus, because, once through the doors of the grand entrance of Europe's largest and busiest court (10,000 cases a month went under the gavel!), you are met with two lines of people. On one side, the wretched and the poor of greater Glasgow awaiting their cases to call, or loved ones to emerge from the many courts in the grand building. Directly opposite them a long line of gowned lawyers giving and taking instructions on their mobile phones. The sight was always slightly surreal.

Running down the line, the cleats of my cycling shoes clacking on the marble floor, I would crash theatrically through the doors of the Sheriff

Clerk's office at the bottom of the grand hallway. The paperwork would be waiting for me to fill out and sign, along with a new court date to be agreed and logged. Then I was off again, skidding along the gauntlet of inequality, out through the revolving doors and onto the bike with a nod to its temporary guardians before peddling back over the suspension bridge into town. Next stop – the well-known firm of Sheriff Officers and Messenger-at-Arms, sited on Royal Exchange Square, a company who made a good living from the medieval structures that still dominated legal life in contemporary Scotland. On many occasions I'd bound up the stairs with seconds to spare and proudly serve the Minute for Recall of the decree for eviction. One of the secretaries (always young, always female) would take the minute through to one of the Sheriff Officers who would phone whoever had been dispatched to oversee the eviction and that, as they say, would be that. The Sheriff Officer present at the property would thus inform the housing officers that the Minute for Recall had duly been served and that the eviction would no longer be taking place. It really was no skin off their nose. They got paid whether the eviction went ahead or not.

As well as preventing homelessness, another of Shelter's roles is education and awareness raising. The staff at Shelter are required to give talks to a wide range of groups as well as deliver training in the rights of tenants and homeless people and the responsibilities of local authorities and the state. The kind of organisations that benefit from such training are Women's Aid, Social Work Departments, Citizen's Advice Bureaux, Immigration and Refugee charities and a wide range of support organisations that provide services to groups that are homeless or at risk of becoming homeless. When the UK's largest stock transfer agreement required Glasgow City Council to hand all of its 88,000 units of accommodation over to the Glasgow Housing Association, the council still had the statutory obligation to provide settled accommodation to those for whom it had an obligation (but no houses to meet their duties). The council had to set up ten separate teams to deal with homeless applications across the city. Shelter were asked to deliver a one-week-long training session to each of the ten newly-formed homelessness case-work teams. The training was comprehensive, and, despite past legal wrangles, was in the main, largely well received.

Not only did Shelter have the expert legal knowledge required to deliver such training, they had a working knowledge and awareness of who knew what and in which areas there were insufficient levels of knowledge. The case-work system that structured their daily contact with clients was the perfect barometer for the gaps in knowledge that would lead to 'bad' and in some cases 'unlawful' practices.

Reflections 3

At Shelter, two problems existed, one in which the issue was 'bad' or 'unlawful' practices, the other was down to structural issues caused by policy and practice failings. Sometimes it was a combination of both. Assignation, a legal procedure that involves a secure tenant assigning the tenancy to someone who was already living there as part of their household, cannot be unreasonably refused. Not only was this an excellent mechanism for preventing the other members of the household becoming homeless, it strengthened communities and gave them stability. However, housing officers would often refuse them because they saw this as 'queue jumping'. These kinds of problems were down to poor practice and were easily resolved as training issues.

Other issues existed that were more difficult to address because they were embedded in the space between well-meaning legislation and a lack of suitable accommodation. An example would be 'overcrowding'. The issue had a disproportionate effect on large families who would come to us for help. I dealt with very many cases where families had five, six, sometimes even seven children. These cases present a significant problem for social housing providers. I'd phone the council or housing association and they'd say, 'we no longer have houses with five bedrooms'. I'd say, 'But the family are currently living in two bedrooms'. Then the housing officer would say, 'Our biggest houses only have four bedrooms and that would mean the property would be statutorily overcrowded, since they require, by law, five bedrooms'. And so an impasse has been reached. Because there are no five-bedroom properties, the family would be stuck in an overcrowded two-bedroom property, simply because giving them four bedrooms would constitute unlawful practice. This is an example of the difficult-to-resolve issues that were rooted in the enmeshing of well-meaning legislative measures and a lack of adequate housing. It's just one of a great many examples in which everything seems crazy.

Comprehensive legal training made good sense to everyone. For homeless people and those who were badly housed it meant that their legal rights to accommodation were properly met. For the local authority case-work teams, it gave them the tools to meet their statutory obligations and for Shelter and other legal centres dealing with housing issues, it meant less appeals and legal interventions. It was a win-win-win situation.

Not all institutions were so easily informed. The private rented sector (PRS), the landlords and letting agents, largely knew little about the arcane and often obscure legislative prescriptions enshrined in housing law in the various jurisdictions across the UK. As highlighted above, protection from summary eviction is an important aspect of housing law but its enforcement is difficult, unless the tenant has some awareness of what a landlord can or cannot do. The law was clear. Failure to follow the prescribed procedures would result in the landlord being guilty of an illegal eviction. Illegal evictions are a criminal offence in all countries of the UK. In Scotland this was enshrined in the *Rent (Scotland) Act 1984*.

Chapter 2 will deal more extensively with the legal context behind evictions but as mentioned above, these rights have been enshrined in law for a very long time. The *Law of Leases 1449* introduces the notion of tacit relocation. This means that if no one brings a fixed term tenancy contract to an end within the correct period (normally two months before the end date) then it continues, automatically, for another full period, until either the landlord or the tenant issues a written termination that follows due process and includes the prescribed information and is issued within the correct timescales. However, too many landlords and letting agency staff think that they can ask the tenants to leave when the tenancy expires. There has been a raft of recent interventions from the legislator to make it more difficult to evict tenants, but to be clear, it was never 'straightforward' in the first place. Illegal evictions are, unfortunately, all too common.

Reflections 4

Legal evictions never made sense to me. They always cost the landlord more than the lost rent, and there were the social costs, particularly if there were kids in the household. But illegal evictions? They were even more difficult to get your head around. The most baffling aspect was trying to get the police to take them seriously. I had the relevant section of the Rent (Scotland) Act 1984 at hand, and would fax it to the relevant desk sergeant whenever the police were called (by the landlord) to make sure the tenants left peacefully. I would phone first and explain that the police officer was aiding and abetting a criminal offence, and that rather than assist with the illegal eviction, the police should be preventing it. I would fax through the relevant section of the Act so the desk sergeant would be in no doubt as to the legal position.

I spent years getting nowhere with this approach. I made official complaints, I contacted senior figures in criminal justice, I wrote to the relevant politicians, and got nowhere. No one was interested. Then one day, I had a client on the phone, it was the usual scenario. I asked to be put onto the police. It was male officer. I informed him that he was aiding and abetting a criminal offence. I gave him my spiel, but he wasn't having any of it, so I phoned his desk sergeant and demanded he take action. I was, as usual, fobbed off. I immediately lodged a complaint. An hour or so later the police officer and his rather embarrassed looking partner turned up to 'have a chat' and 'sort it out'. I fetched the Act and tried my best to convince them that they were acting unlawfully. The officer started by saying that there was no rent book, and thus no tenancy, therefore no 'illegal' eviction. I showed him another Act that prescribed the four elements of a lease, the requirements being; parties (landlord and tenant), period (length of time in tenancy), subject (house or flat) and rent (monies paid). 'Ah!' he said, 'but it's a furnished flat, and furnished flats don't count'.

I showed him the legislation that busted the myth about furnished flats having less security of tenure than unfurnished ones. He then told me with enormous confidence that the landlord's rights always trump those of the tenant. Exasperated I took the time to show him that this assessment could not be further from the truth. I then resorted to the broken record technique. I pointed to the relevant part of the Act and repeatedly said 'a criminal offence, a criminal offence, a criminal offence, A CRIMINAL OFFENCE!' The policeman put his hand on my shoulder and said, patronisingly, 'You see ... what it is, is ...' I could see his colleague lowering her head in embarrassment. 'You see, some crimes are crimes, and some crimes arnae[1] crimes'. So, having had enough, I unceremoniously evicted them both from the office.

Up until I began working at Shelter in 2000, the legislative frameworks that governed housing and homelessness across the countries of the UK, were broadly speaking very similar, as many aspects had been brought into alignment. It was in 1997 however that the people of Scotland voted for devolution and following the *Scotland Act 1998*, the Scottish Parliament was established in 1999 and there was significant divergence in the overall package of rights afforded to the populations in the north and south of the UK. One of the very first things the newly formed Scottish Parliament did was to set up the Homelessness Task Force in August 1999. The remit of the Task Force was to take a serious look at the issues surrounding homelessness and its causes and make a wide range of recommendations, the aim of which was to eradicate homelessness altogether. The Director of Shelter was a key figure in this Task Force and Shelter actively campaigned for better legal and regulatory powers to assist local authorities and other landlords in tackling the issue of homelessness in Scotland. By 2001, the group had made 59 recommendations, from which a raft of legislative innovations emerged.

One of the most 'radical' was the *Homelessness Etc. (Scotland) Act 2003*,[2] which initially saw the abolition of three of the four 'hurdles' in what was the sequential test to determine whether or not the local authority to which an applicant presented had a statutory duty to accommodate them. This meant that if a person was homeless, the following three hurdles would be removed, these were; 'priority need', 'intentionality' and 'local connection'. This innovation, something for which Shelter had been campaigning for many years, removed the most significant barriers to social rented accommodation, while at the same time, removing the stigma of a tenure that was reserved for those who had members of their household who were vulnerable or had special 'needs'.

The general thinking behind the wholesale removal of the barriers to social housing can be found in the Chancellor Gordon Brown's rhetorical pronouncements that we had reached an end of boom and bust economics. This was, he claimed, a period where compound growth would continue unfettered, and where the housing market would remain buoyant while the ever-expanding mortgage market would extend its reach to include more and more of those groups previously excluded from homeownership. The desire was that, as more and more people realized their 'dream' of homeownership and moved out of social housing, more units would be freed up, so that anyone who was homeless, would be entitled to a home. The ambitious recommendations of the Homelessness Task force were severely watered down immediately following the global banking crash of 2008. The plan to ensure that everyone who was homeless had a right to settled accommodation was reduced to the abolition of priority need, with the need to prove you had a local connection to that authority being kept in place but being downgraded from being a 'duty' to being a 'power' over which councils had discretion to apply or not. Progress, but nowhere nearly as far reaching as first envisioned.

In the early to mid-2000s, despite the sums of money that were spent on what the Labour Party called 'social inclusion' initiatives, it was clear the state's right hand, its disciplining and punishing institutions were beginning to colonise the welfare and social inclusion functions of the state. In its first nine years, Blair's government had created more than 3000 new criminal offences, one for almost every day it had been in power. The criminalisation of nuisance emerged as a new policy objective and new laws were introduced to tackle 'anti-social behaviour'. The Anti-Social Behaviour Order (ASBO) was an attempt to encourage active citizenship through the modification of behaviour, such as 'responsibilisation', and the threat of stigmatization for non-compliance. People could now be evicted, or were threatened with eviction, because of their lifestyle-behaviours or those of their children. The new age of punitive paternalism was emerging from the criminalising laws of a Labour Party that had, in past reincarnations, been known for their progressive policies. Under New Labour, the caring 'nanny state' that it so famously constructed, was replaced by the disciplinary 'daddy state'. These were seismic social policy transitions that created more and more layers of complexity around eviction practices, making them even more difficult to understand, at least from a commonsense perspective.

Reflections 5

Some days change your life forever. I remember this one very clearly. It was Shelter's annual conference in Glasgow. The morning before, myself and a few dozen other anti-nuclear protesters had been arrested, having mechanically fastened ourselves to each other and blocked the gates of Faslane Naval Base, the permanent home of The Trident Submarine fleet. Once the police had cut through the metal pipes and eventually managed to remove the chains from our arms, we were lifted off the rain-soaked road and taken to various police stations in Glasgow to be processed and charged. The next morning my brother in law picked me up after a restless night on a hard-plastic mattress, and I had just enough time to get home, shower and change in time for the conference in Glasgow's City Chambers. Its marble opulence (an interior that film-makers use as a 'body-double' for the Winter Palace in St Petersburg) could not have provided more of a contrast to my previous night's accommodation.

After a number of fairly dull talks and a fancy finger-buffet lunch, Professor Peter Kemp from the University of Glasgow presented his recent research for the Scottish Government. The title was 'The Structural Causes of Homelessness' and in that single 45-minute talk, he articulated all the questions that I had been chewing over since I started at Shelter. Wow. A light went on. I wanted more of this. I wanted to understand what he understood. I wanted the knowledge and ability to dissect the causes of social problems the way he did; comprehensively, theoretically and critically. The most remarkable thing is that the very next day I did a spin class in the gym near our office, showered and then unusually for me, jumped into the jacuzzi. I did a double-take as I splashed into the bubbly water and startled the man beside me. 'Are you Professor Kemp?' He nodded warily, so I told him how much of an impact his presentation had made, asked him some questions that resulted in him suggesting that I give consideration to doing a part-time MPhil in Urban Studies at Glasgow. So I did. And it changed my life.

Although the Labour party spent record sums of money on tackling a wide range of social problems, the encroachment of the state's surveillance and disciplinary mechanisms into its welfare function resulted in what Berkley Professor Loic Wacquant (2009) called the double-regulation of the poor. Add to this the unprecedented levels of re-regulation and deregulation in favour of banks and businesses, and the boom years became unsustainable. As more and more wealthy individuals diverted their taxable revenue into off shore secrecy jurisdictions, the newly formed Glasgow Housing Association (the GHA) were ramping up their efforts to recover rent arrears that had accrued under the council's tenure. A massive demolition programme was also initiated, one that saw over 30,000 units, almost all of them in high-rise or tenement accommodation, being pulled down. Entire areas in Glasgow, such as the Gorbals and Partick were extensively gentrified as their former residents were relocated to the remaining schemes, many of which were in low demand areas.

Shelter, too, was undergoing its own transformation. An influx of new senior managers replaced the old guard and before long celebrity endorsements, corporate rebranding and organisational restructuring was being rolled out across Shelter's UK operations. This meant a contraction in service provision, job losses through project closure and an end to what had been a decade of continuous augmentation in working conditions and financial remuneration. Labour relations deteriorated and the union went into long-term dispute with management, a process that was referred to The Advisory, Conciliation and Arbitration Service (ACAS).

Reflections 6

Evictions were on the rise, rogue landlords were on the rampage and the availability of housing stock was at an all time low. The global banking collapse wrought chaos in the sector and the so-called credit crunch led to a massive contraction in services accompanied by devastating job losses all through the public and private sectors. After almost a decade of fighting – the last few years on two fronts – I was burned out. A particularly difficult day in the office after I had to phone a housing officer back and apologise for insulting him in our previous conversation, lead to my boss leaving an open copy of national newspaper, The Herald, on my desk. The job advert she had circled said 'Teaching Fellow in Housing Studies, University of Stirling'. I looked at it and thought, wow, now that would be amazing. I tossed the paper back onto the top of my in-tray. They wouldn't give something like that, to someone like me, would they? I'd blagged my way into Shelter, but it was entirely on merit that I'd got myself an MPhil in Urban Studies while I was there. Could I blag my way into an academic post as well? Of course I could! I was sad to leave the cut and thrust of the front-line at Shelter, but it was my time to go. On my last day I was heartened when I opened my case management system and ran a report on all my closed cases. I tallied the number of evictions I had successfully prevented. Although the outcomes of some of them were difficult to determine, and the results sometimes unclear, the system showed the number was over 500.

This is where the book's journey begins. Having spent almost a decade fighting landlords, local authority housing officers, housing association managers, councillors, letting agents and anyone else who represented an obstacle to the full attainment of my client's housing rights, it was time to change direction. My initial concern was that in making the transition from practice to academia, I would be removed completely from the front-line and placed in an ivory tower away from the action. Not so. My first taste of pedagogical action involved teaching the Diploma in Housing Studies (accredited by the Chartered Institute for Housing) to around 40 full time housing professionals on day release. Although I was not dealing directly with clients, the fight for social justice took on a different character and continued under a different set of circumstances. The relationship between myself and the housing profession went from one which was often fraught with tension and animosity and in which conflict and confrontation were never far away, to one in which we shared knowledge and ideas while calmly discussing bad practice at the break over coffee and cake. The change in relationship also gave me an entirely different perspective.

On everything.

Notes

1 Arnea = 'are not' in the Glaswegian vernacular.
2 This is the correct title of the Act.

References

Bourdieu P. and Wacquant L. (1992) *An Invitation to Reflexive Sociology*, London: Polity.

Desmond M. (2016) *Evictions: Poverty and Profit in the American City*, London: Penguin.

Lancione M. (2017) 'A început ploaia/It started raining: Fighting for the right to housing in Bucharest'. https://vimeo.com/205064103.

Preece J. (2018) *The Impact of Welfare and Tenancy Reforms on Housing Associations. An Evidence Review*, UK Centre for Collaborative Evidence.

Wacquant L. (2009) *Punishing the Poor: The Neoliberal Government of Social Insecurity*, Durham: Duke University Press.

Wilson W. (2019) *Housing Costs in Universal Credit*, Briefing Paper Number 6547, 8 May 2019, House of Commons Library.

2 The Legal and Regulatory Context

Exposition

Since this is a book about the housing professionals who carry out evictions and their practices, it is necessary to proceed with a much broader view of the legal and regulatory framework that underpin the processes and the procedures that govern evictions. By locating evictions within a wider context, it is possible to stand back and observe the political processes that have driven the interventions that shape the legal and regulatory landscape. The political dimension of evictions will be addressed in Chapter 3. This chapter, will highlight the main areas of the legal and regulatory framework to which housing professionals in both the social and private housing sectors are subject.

Beginning with the historical context, this chapter will show the extent to which current legal requirements have a long history, with many originating in the medieval period, before the United Kingdom was formed by the *1707 Treaty of Union*. The laws that govern residential tenancies and security of tenure represent an arcane area of jurisprudence that is hardly understood outside the specialist field of housing law. This complexity, alongside the space restrictions imposed by the book, mean that only a very general overview can be provided here. This broad-brush approach aims to provide the reader with a very rough map in order to set the direction of travel and to appreciate the significance of the legislative interventions and policies facilitating regulatory oversight.

Another area of interest will be the introduction of rights for homeless people. Having an indirect effect on evictions, this is significant since it places a statutory duty upon local authorities to temporarily accommodate those forcibly removed from their home, and where there are vulnerable members of the household such as children, to provide settled accommodation. The inception of the Scottish Parliament and the devolution of housing as an area of legal competence means that Scotland now continues, as it did before 1707, to provide one of the most progressive packages of rights for both tenants and homeless persons in Europe. Developments in the private rented sector (PRS) are also of great significance because of the two-way relationship between evictions and the PRS. Not only do the majority of evictions come from private tenancies, the PRS is also used to re-accommodate those who have been evicted by social landlords. As well as the legislative landscape that governs residential tenancies in both the social and private sectors, this chapter will take a brief look at the regulatory framework within which housing professionals and landlords must operate. This is of significance as it shapes, perhaps more than the legislative framework, the everyday practices that govern evictions.

Evictions are a social phenomenon. They are governed by rules and regulations, laws and legal procedures, professional codes of conduct and codified conventions. Eviction, as a form of professional practice, is therefore an assemblage of social, political and legal constructions. These constructions are political insofar as they arise from the struggles between powerful groups vying for the monopoly over the legitimate right to define social problems and to say what should be done about them. It is prudent to point out that evictions are always and at all times underpinned by a range of power relations. The relation between the landlord and tenant, as well as being a lopsided relation of power, is fundamentally a legal relation. It is defined in statute. It is governed by law.

One of the key objects of study in this book is the relationship between landlord and tenant in both the public and private spheres in the UK. The issues that underpin the mortgage market sector, a field that implies a relationship between lender and borrower are not the concern of this book. 'Repossessions' and 'foreclosures' have in common with evictions the fact that they mostly result in homelessness, but this is a book, not about homelessness as such, but about evictions.

The Historical Context

Because the UK is made up of four countries, it is not accurate to say that there exists such a thing as UK housing policy, or a unified UK housing system (see McKee et al., 2017). What is certain is that it there is no such entity as UK housing law. When the Acts of Union were signed between the Kingdoms of Scotland and England in 1707, it was agreed that Scotland would maintain its independence in matters of law and religion. Despite having distinct legal systems after the treaty of union was signed, matters such as housing law were, particularly in the 20th century, guided by the principles laid down by Westminster. This created a much greater homogeneity in the general direction of travel in UK housing policy from the middle of the twentieth century, when programmes for the mass building of social housing were adopted by both Conservative and Labour governments.

The Scottish Parliament took over full legislative control of housing after Devolution in 1999. This has given tenants in Scotland one of the strongest packages of rights in the European Union (EU), a framework that England and Wales are beginning to adopt. Housing legislation within Scots law has a rather longer history than England and Wales. Indeed, much of this historical development is still evident in the package of rights enjoyed throughout the United Kingdom. Today, tenants who are in private rented accommodation will not have to renew their lease at the end of the fixed term period, on the grounds that it *tacitly relocates* to the next period and does so *ad infinitum*, until one of the parties, landlord or tenant, brings the tenancy to an end. This notion of '*tacit relocation*' originates from the *Leases Act of 1449*, passed by the Parliament of Scotland. This same Act also protects the security of tenure of sitting tenants when the property changes hands, just as it does today.

The law governing evictions in both the social and private rented sectors, having evolved over many centuries, represents one of the most arcane areas of legislation in an already difficult to understand juridical field. The first statutory regulation and protection of tenants in eviction cases has been prescribed in statute since as long ago as the *Act of 1555*. This was passed by the Parliament of Scotland "to rid the country of the violence which was a usual accompaniment to the older removings ... on verbal warnings only" (Rankin, 1916: 550 quoted in Stalker, 2007: 4). The 40-day notice period emerged from the 1555 Act that also stated that failure of the tenant to heed such notice could result in the landlord seeking a legal remedy in the form of a decree for eviction in the Sheriff Court. Once the decree had been granted, the "landlord had then to apply directly to the local Sheriff for a warrant of ejection" (Stalker, 2007: 4). What seems remarkable about this early form of eviction procedure is that the two foundational aspects have survived to be very much part of eviction proceedings today. There is still a requirement to issue notices, and there is still a legal requirement to acquire a decree from the sheriff court (or a court order in England and Wales), the granting of which requires that a Sheriff Officer (or bailiff in England) be instructed to oversee the eviction itself. The law governing eviction changed only slightly between the 1555 Act and the *Sheriff Courts (Scotland) Act 1907* which provided the means by which the decree for removing and the warrant for ejection could be obtained as part of the same single process (Stalker, 2007). Today, the procedures for eviction are similar in England and Wales since they have been adopted and incorporated into housing law over the centuries, developing into the comprehensive package of rights that currently exist in the UK.

These legislative measures should not be regarded simply as either progressive or pragmatic, since they are both at the same time. While *Leases Act of 1449* and the *Act of 1555* provides security of tenure to tenants, which is of great benefit to them, as historian Jim Hunter (2015) points out, it was not in the landlord's interests for either the land or the property to be left waste. Housing rights always had a twofold truth, since they were of benefit to both the landlord class as well as giving tenants better and stronger rights. This twofold political truth underpinning the development of housing law, applies as much to the legislative interventions of today as it does to those of the late middle ages.

As the industrial period concentrated large populations into the main industrial cities, the private rental market in the UK was also subject to some radical state interventions. The Glasgow Rent Strikes of 1915 resulted in swift action from Westminster to legislate to control rents throughout the UK at a time of war. From 1915 until the *Housing Act of 1988*, private renting was regulated through a series of evolving Rent Acts. The Conservative Government under Prime Minister Margaret Thatcher brought rent controls to an end in its attempts to stimulate the private rental market, replacing the system of 'fair rents' with the notion of 'market rent'. It was not until the global banking crash of 2008 and the return of the rentier capitalist,[1] that the private rented sector recovered to become the tenure it once was, one hundred years previously.

The Rent Acts which followed the 1915 Act also covered the issue of illegal eviction making it a criminal offence (in a field governed almost exclusively by civil law) to evict or to threaten to evict any tenant without first obtaining a decree for eviction from a sheriff court. Having existed for a mere 100 years, social housing is, in relative terms, a very recent phenomenon. As such, it is clear that the legal prescriptions that formed the foundations of the package of rights enjoyed by tenants of social landlords had their origins in the rights historically bestowed upon private sector tenants. It was not until the 1970s however, that the extensive package of rights that protect households from homelessness emerged from a series of economic and social crises.

Homelessness Rights

The first significant Act to introduce statutory duties on social landlords in the UK, placing upon them obligations to provide accommodation for those in housing need, was the *Housing (Homeless Persons) Act 1977*. The prescriptions of this early legislative attempt to statutorily enshrine housing rights for those in housing need, were consolidated in the *Housing (Scotland) Act 1987* and the *Housing Act 1996 (England and Wales)*, both of which set out the duties of local authorities in meeting their statutory obligations towards homeless people and those who were threatened with homelessness. These Acts were significant as they introduced the four sequential tests, meaning that a local authority had a duty to accommodate if the household was:

- Homeless (they have no accommodation in the UK)
- In priority need (they have children or other vulnerabilities)
- Unintentionally homeless (they made themselves homeless through their own actions or inactions)
- They have a local connection (once the first three are established the last test is simply to determine who has the duty to provide settled accommodation)

The social effect of this was also significant. By introducing a system of rationing, the general character of social housing was altered significantly.

By removing the universality of local authority housing and turning this type of tenure into a 'needs-based' form in which vulnerability was privileged, social housing went from being the dominant tenure of choice for workers, to a stigmatised tenure for those in greatest 'need'.

As political and economic priorities shifted in the 1980s the legislative changes to the private rented sector meant that protections were shifted from this tenure, onto that of the needs-based social tenure. The introduction of the *Housing Act 1988*, and its counterpart, the *Housing (Scotland) Act 1988*, was significant in so far as it radically tilted the balance of power towards the landlord. This diminished the tenant's rights to stay, as well as their rights to 'fair rents', and augmented the landlord's ability to issue short fixed-term tenancies, as well as furnishing the landlord with the ability to bring the tenancy to an end at a prescribed point of the lease. As long as the landlord followed the correct procedures as prescribed in the 1988 Act, then they could terminate the tenancy without reason, as well as being free to raise the rent, a process that had been limited under the previous system of rent control. This reregulation of the PRS was made possible because the social safety net, provided by the needs-based character of homeless legislation, could absorb the fallout in cases involving families with children and/or other vulnerable members of the household. Single persons, who were not deemed to have a vulnerability, were fully expected to utilise the PRS, either on a permanent basis or until they could afford the deposit for a mortgage.

Single persons or couples without children were gradually being excluded from social housing. However, as mechanisms were introduced to expand the mortgage market to an increasing number of those who had previously been excluded, homeownership continued to rise. Government backed interventions such as the Right to Buy (your council house), Help to Buy, Mortgage Interest Relief, and Shared Ownership all helped millions of families get onto the so-called 'property ladder'.

Devolution for Scotland

The Scotland Act of 1998 granted Scotland its own devolved parliament and entailed the devolution of housing and housing law to the newly formed parliament at Holyrood. The immediate formation of the Homelessness Taskforce resulted in a number of recommendations, leading to a raft of new Housing Acts that promised Scotland the most progressive package of homelessness rights in Europe (Anderson and Serpa, 2013). The 59 recommendations made by the Task force were, due to changes in the UK's economic situation, significantly reduced. Despite this dilution, what resulted was still characterised as one of the most comprehensive packages of rights in the world. The initial aim was to improve access to housing through the removal of the barriers to accommodation represented by the sequential test mentioned above. The central idea was simple. If a person was homeless, then they would have a statutory right to suitable settled accommodation, without the need to prove eligibility or scrutiny for evidence that they had made themselves homeless intentionally. That the local authority would have an 'unending duty' towards homeless persons, was the key objective of the recommendations of the Taskforce.

The first Act to be passed by the Scottish Parliament was the *Housing (Scotland) Act 2001*. As well as updating the package of rights that tenants enjoyed, it also created a uniformity of tenure between housing associations which previously had assured tenancies and council tenants who had secure tenancies. The 2001 Act aligned them both, a measure which was essential in facilitating the large-scale transfer of housing stock from local authorities to housing associations. In 2002, Glasgow tenants voted in favour of stock transfer and some 88,000 properties were taken over by the newly formed Glasgow Housing Association (GHA).

The enactment of the *Homelessness Etc. (Scotland) Act 2003* [sic] was intended to herald in some of the recommendations of the Task Force, revolutionising housing and ending homelessness. As well as expanding the categories of those who would be eligible for assistance, the 2003 Act focused on the prevention of homelessness with, in particular, Section 11 summarised by Shelter in the following passage:

> Mortgage lenders, private landlords and/or registered social landlords (RSLs) must inform the relevant LA when they initiate legal proceedings to repossess a property. The early warning that a Section 11 notification provides should allow for information and support to be provided to households, which will prevent homelessness occurring, or will allow a planned approach for suitable alternative accommodation to be found.
>
> (Shelter, 2009)

As alluded to above, the plan to implement the world's most progressive housing and homelessness legislation was entirely predicated on continued growth in both the wider economy and the housing market. The early signs were good. Although it had begun to slow, homeownership levels did continue to increase throughout the first decade of the millennium, as more and more government initiatives were introduced, expanding the market to include more and more groups who had previously been unable to obtain a mortgage. If homeownership continued to increase then more social rented stock would be made available as more people transitioned to homeownership. Of course, this period of uninterrupted if slowing economic growth was not to last.

As the global banking collapse placed the ambitious aims of the Task Force under question, concessions ensued, and the recommendations were diluted. Without the available housing stock, the plans to place an unending duty upon local authorities to accommodate everyone who was statutorily homeless was revised. First to go was the third sequential test of 'intentionality'. By preserving this test any tenant deemed by the local authority to "have done or have failed to have done something, the consequence of which was that they lost their accommodation, which was reasonable for them to occupy", would have made themselves intentionally homeless, relieving the local authority of its duty to provide settled accommodation. This single aspect of the dilution of the Taskforce's 59 recommendations had, by some considerable way, the most detrimental effect on the key aim of ensuring that there was an unending duty towards homeless persons. It also had a serious effect on the potential to make evictions for rent arrears a thing of the past.

In England, no such plan to remove any of the four sequential tests emerged, instead Parliament issued *The Homelessness (Priority Need for Accommodation) (England) Order 2002*. When Scotland was in the process of abolishing the priority need category, England and Wales took steps to clarify who was and who was not in priority need of housing, thus embedding the policy within a more robust legal framework.

The Welsh Assembly, set up in 1999, was given voting powers in 2011 allowing Wales to pass its first ever housing Act in 2014. The introduction of the *Housing (Wales) Act 2014* and the *Renting Homes (Wales) Act 2016*, set Wales apart from England for the first time, moving them closer to Scotland in their attempt to install a comprehensive package of rights in order to address the old 'rationing' system where only the most vulnerable had a right to assistance.

The Housing (Scotland) Act 2010

The Housing (Scotland) Act 2010 was passed by the Scottish Parliament on 3 November 2010. As well as creating the Scottish Housing Regulator (which will be discussed below) the Act introduced some important amendments to the *Housing (Scotland) Act 2001* which affected any registered social landlord (RSL) who sought to raise eviction proceedings against a tenant on the grounds of rent arrears. There were 75,000 actions raised against social tenants in Scotland in 2010/11 (Shelter, 2012). Shelter had long voiced concerns that actions were being raised unnecessarily and prematurely and campaigned for the creation and implementation of some form of checklist with which RSLs must comply before resorting to court action. Following consultation, the government amended Section 14 of the *Housing (Scotland) Act 2001* that now carries the requirement of an RSL to have complied with the prescriptions of section 14A of the 2001 Act when raising an action on the grounds of rent arrears in terms of paragraph 1 of Schedule 2 of the same Act.

The lists of measures, also known as the Pre-Action Requirements are as follows:

- The landlord must provide the tenant with clear information about the terms of the tenancy agreement together with any outstanding rent and any other financial obligation of the tenancy;

- The landlord must make reasonable efforts to provide the tenant with advice and assistance on the tenant's eligibility to receive housing benefit and other types of financial assistance;
- The landlord must provide the tenant with information about sources of advice and assistance in relation to management of debt;
- The landlord must make reasonable efforts to agree with the tenant a reasonable plan for future payments to the landlord, this plan must include proposals in respect of future payments of rent, outstanding rent and any other financial obligations of the tenancy;
- The landlord must not serve a Notice of Proceedings if an application for housing benefit for the tenant has been made (but not yet determined) and is, in the landlord's opinion, likely to result in benefit being paid at a level which would allow the tenant to pay, or reduce by an amount acceptable to the landlord, the outstanding rent and any other financial obligation of the tenancy;
- The landlord must not serve a Notice of Proceedings if the tenant is taking other steps which, in the opinion of the landlord, are likely to result in payment within a reasonable timescale of the outstanding rent and any other outstanding financial obligation of the tenancy. Or the tenant is complying with a repayment plan agreed with the landlord;
- The landlord must encourage the tenant to contact the local authority in whose area the house is situated.

The *Housing (Scotland) Act 2010* prescribes that a decree (termination of tenancy order) no longer ends the tenancy; it will only be ended once the RSL or local authority recovers possession. That means that the tenant still has the implied right to occupy the property until duly removed by the Sheriff Officers. This, it is hoped, will resolve a number of issues pertaining to situations where landlords obtain decree then allow tenants to remain in their tenancy while payments are being made. Third sector organisations and tenant's groups have long criticised landlords for what they see as the misuse of a procedure for the purposes of rent collection. The Act also recommends that the decree specifies a time period within which the RSL can recover possession, thereby addressing the question of how long a decree remains enforceable. The time scale is set out by the Housing Minister. This amendment only applies to Paragraph 1 of the *Housing (Scotland) Act 2001*, which deals with rent arrears.

Similar in spirit to the *Housing (Scotland) Act 2010*, the Westminster Parliament passed *The Homelessness Reduction Act 2017*. This bolted-on two new duties to the original statutory obligations retained by local authorities. The first was the introduction of a 'duty' to prevent homelessness and the second introduced a 'duty' to relieve homelessness. Although England did not abolish 'priority need', it exempted the category in respect of a local authority's duties under the Homelessness Prevention Act 2017, a measure that came into force on April 2018. This meant that that English Authorities had a duty to take early intervention measures in order to prevent homelessness from occurring, irrespective of the personal status regarding 'priority need'.

Regulation and Inspection

As well as giving landlords more obligations to reduce the numbers of evictions for rent arrears, the *Housing (Scotland) Act 2010* created the Scottish Housing Regulator replacing 'Communities Scotland' as the body that regulates and inspects the social housing sector, regulating 180 Registered Social Landlords (RSLs) as well as the 32 Scottish local authorities. In their own words they say that "Our statutory objective is to safeguard and promote the interests of current and future tenants, homeless people and others who use services provided by social landlords" (Scottish Housing Regulator, 2016).

What is curious about this claim is that despite the emphasis on promoting the interests of tenants, the Scottish Housing Regulator's work is almost exclusively based on business models, performance standards, and measured outcomes of landlords:

> Each year we ask all registered social landlords to send us information that shows us how they have performed against the standards and outcomes of the Scottish Social Housing Charter. We use this information to produce our reports, for tenants, about their landlord's performance.
>
> (Scottish Housing Regulator, 2016)

The Scottish Housing Regulator's website offers readers a drop-down section entitled *Find and Compare Landlords*, which contains a wide range of statistical data on a number of key performance indicators. The page offers links to various sources and data sets including a spread sheet set with multiple sets of benchmarking tables, 14 financial tables and nine performance tables.

Eight years after the Scottish Parliament augmented its regulatory function by passing the *Housing (Scotland) Act 2010*, England, in 2018 replaced the Homes and Communities Agency with Homes England and the Regulator of Social Housing. January 2019, saw the publication of its list of Regulatory Standards, these comprised a set of Economic Standards as well as a set of Consumer Standards. The Three Economic Standards were Governance and Financial Viability, Value for Money, and Rent. Both regulatory bodies took the same approach. The entire framework clearly has an emphatic focus on the 'financial' aspects of housing provision. There are of course some 'tenant-focused' standards but even these are couched in the language of consumer rights, with an emphasis on empowering tenants in their ability to ensure their landlords are providing housing services to an adequate standard.

The Private Rented Sector

The global banking collapse of 2008[2] had many consequences, a number of which had repercussions on other sectors of the housing system. Once it was agreed to retain the test of 'intentionality', the removal, scheduled for 2012, of the 'priority need' category, would still have far reaching consequences for local authorities that had built very few, if any, units of accommodation since the Right to Buy your council house became popular in the early 1980s. Not only did the collapse of lending and the concomitant demise of the mortgage market revive the private rented sector (PRS), the pressure on social housing stock, from legislation that widened access to it at a time of economic buoyancy, led to the PRS reasserting itself as a significant tenure after almost a century at the margins.

Even before the worst of the so-called austerity measures were implemented after the 2008 banking crisis, there was recognition that there would be a need to increase existing housing options and, in fitting with the third-way agenda of the then Labour government, the private rented sector was, for a number of reasons, the obvious choice for this expansion. This, however, was not without its challenges. The Private Rented Sector (PRS) in the UK was one of the most under-regulated in Europe and a combination of substandard conditions coupled with an awareness of the high prevalence of poor practices among the landlord fraternity (Kemp, 2004), led to the drafting of what was to become the *Housing (Scotland) Act 2006*. This legislative intervention dealt almost exclusively with the PRS and effectively addressed a large number of concerns ranging from the tenants' right to repair, robust enforcement mechanisms, as well as tenancy deposit regulation, a 'fit and proper person' test, and a register for landlords.

Leading the way once more, the Scottish Government introduced the *Housing (Scotland) Act 2014*, a legislative measure that not only abolished the Right to Buy in the social housing sector but introduced the wide range of measures that would address the remaining problems associated with private renting. The main focus of this Act was to deal with the repair issues, facilitating a housing tribunal approach that allowed tenants to be able to adequately deal with landlords who refused to carry out repairs. It placed the onus on the tenant to take the landlord to the Private Rented Housing Panel, an independent body that had the powers to enforce and ensure that repairs were done. The main mechanism for doing this was the imposition of rent abatement orders when landlords refused to comply on time. The significant loss of income tended to outweigh the cost of doing essential repairs and even the most unscrupulous of landlords found themselves in a position where they were much more likely to carry out repairs.

In the Private Rented Sector, right across the UK, measures have been introduced to bring this tenure closer to the standards enjoyed by its European neighbours. There is no doubt that this has resulted in a wide range of improvements, particularly with regard to the perennial problems of repairs, the right to privacy and the theft of tenancy deposits. Improving standards is one thing, but the impact on de-regulation in the PRS has left a legacy of other problems, particularly in respect of security of tenure.

In England, in the last five years, homelessness has risen by 22%. The loss of a private tenancy remains the single biggest cause of homelessness, with 18,750 households becoming homeless after an eviction from a privately rented home in 2016. Since 2011, the rise in the number of households evicted from a privately rented home has accounted for 78% of the rise in homelessness (Shelter, 2017). In 2017, there were 21,439 possession claims by private landlords using the standard procedure (Section 8 and Section 21). Of these claims, there were 6,260 repossessions under this procedure in 2017, close to the 2014 peak of 6,321 possessions (House of Commons Library, 2018).

In response, Westminster introduced further protections for tenants under the *Enterprise and Regulatory Reform Act 2013* and the *Deregulation Act 2015*, with the latter introducing protections for tenants against retaliatory eviction where they have a legitimate complaint about the condition of the property. This issue, what Shelter calls 'revenge evictions' continued despite the legislative measure to protect tenants (Shelter, 2014). This is a problem that persists, as evidenced by a survey of over 2000 tenants in England by the organisation Citizen's Advice (2018), which found that almost half who had made a complaint regarding essential repairs were at risk of being evicted within six months. At the time of writing there is a consultation process underway in England, the outcome of which may replicate the more radical measures already in Scotland and planned for Wales, to remove the landlords right to evict without reason. The most recent intervention in relation to tackling the issue of property standards is the *Homes (Fitness for Human Habitation) Act 2018*, which came into force in England on 20 March 2019. It is too early to assess the impact of these, the most recent interventions, but what can be said about the regulatory regime in England is that it constitutes a two-pronged approach. First, it seeks to address problems caused by what it terms 'the rogue landlord'; second, it seeks to address the issue of 'standards', particularly in respect of repairs and maintenance.

Not to be outdone, the Welsh Assembly also took radical steps to bring the PRS up to some degree of tolerable standard by passing the *Renting Homes (Wales) Act 2016*. This, a much more ambitious plan than the one passed in England, is more in line with the Scottish system of comprehensive regulation, the aim of which is 'a complete overhaul of the sector' (Ministry of Housing, Communities and Local Government [MHCLG], 2019b). Due to the complexity of the housing situation in Northern Ireland, coupled with the difficulties experienced by Stormont the Northern Ireland Assembly, it has been left out of this analysis.

While the focus on England has been almost exclusively concerned with improving 'standards', Wales and to a much greater extent Scotland have recently taken measures to prevent evictions in the PRS with the possibility to apply rent restrictions. In 2016, the Scottish Government passed the *Private Housing (Tenancies) (Scotland) Act 2016 Act*, outlawing the use of no-fault evictions. On the 1 December 2017, the right of landlords in Scotland to simply end the tenancy once the contractual period had run its course was removed. The tenant would have to breach one of the tenancy conditions in order for the landlord to then take the case to the First Tier Tribunal to seek a decree for eviction. This *Private Housing (Tenancies) (Scotland) Act 2016 Act* also placed Scotland in a unique position in the UK as the only country that can impose rent controls in certain situations, under specific economic conditions. However, these have yet to be implemented, anywhere.

Evaluation – How Has It All Been Working Out?

The second decade of the 21st century saw a raft of the most progressive and comprehensive legislative interventions designed not only to further improve services through an augmentation in regulatory standards, but to protect households from eviction across the UK. Perhaps the most far-reaching of these were in the private rented sector (PRS). The most under-regulated PRS in Europe was, especially in Scotland, brought into the 21st century with a regulatory bang that provided a range of protections in order that the tenure could grow, and offer a real alternative for those who could not afford the deposit for a mortgage and those who didn't meet the criteria for social housing. Repairing standards, procedures to protect tenant's deposits, enforcement measures to ensure tolerable standards, rent abatement orders to force landlords to act, all combined to produce a significant suite of, what looked on paper, to be entirely progressive reforms.

In the social rented sector in all countries of the UK, progressive legislative interventions have made evictions more difficult to carry out than before. In order for the local authority or housing association to repossess their property by removing the household, the tenant has to have breached the terms of the tenancy agreement, and the social landlord has also to prove that eviction really is a last resort, all other interventions and options having been exhausted. But this is not as solid a protection as it first appears. Overwhelmingly, the vast majority of evictions in the UK's social rented sector are for rent arrears (The Ministry of Housing, Communities and Local Government, 2019a).

Beginning with social tenancies in Scotland, if a tenant accrues three months of rent arrears, they will have breached the conditions of their tenancy agreement. This automatically sets in motion the evictions procedure. However, recent legislation means that the local authority or registered social landlord, has to follow all the pre-action requirements before proceeding to court. The Sheriff still has discretion, and in some cases where there are young children, or vulnerable members of the household, the

Sheriff may not grant the decree. However, persistence on the part of the landlord will eventually leave the Sheriff little option but to grant the decree if the rent arrears continue over a protracted period, or if the arrangement to make regular re-payments of the arrears has been broken. No matter how many protective innovations are enacted, no matter how much progressive legislation is passed, no matter the extent to which the landlord has to show that they have exhausted all possible interventions, it takes three month's rent arrears to start a process which, until the money's are recovered, gathers momentum, the outcome of which results in eviction.

Shelter (2019) provided two case studies in their own campaign literature that are representative of the cases they deal with in relation to evictions for rent arrears in Scotland. These are summarised below in order that some idea be provided as to the character of contemporary eviction cases;

Case study 1

A single mother could not cover her local authority rent due to changes to the benefit cap. The woman struggled with managing letters from her local authority about her arrears level and entitlement to benefits as she can't read. The family are now at risk of eviction due to arrears. Shelter Scotland is helping the family apply for discretionary housing payments to help prevent the eviction.

Case study 2

A single mother with a four-year-old son was living in local authority housing and was signed off work with stress. Unfortunately, she was subject to the benefit cap and her income was cut. She applied for a discretionary housing payment twice and was awarded it once when there was money available but refused on another occasion. Her rent arrears accrued to £1,500, at which point the local authority began eviction proceedings. The court granted the eviction.

The Regulation and Inspection regime in its various forms across the UK, prioritises the management of rent arrears in what is clearly a set of financially focused regulatory standards. The other priorities of financial well-being and value for money combined with a clear operational emphasis on the prioritisation of rent collection, result in the prioritisation of an economistic and managerialist approach. This has had very mixed results in respect of evictions.

In England and Wales, the protections from evictions in the social rented sector are less robust than they are in Scotland where the local authority is under obligation to take measures to ensure that evictions are the last resort and that homelessness is, where possible, prevented or alleviated. The rights of tenants in England and Wales are not as comprehensive, and the obligations on landlords nowhere nearly as extensive, as they are in Scotland.

Yet without the augmented list of pre-action requirements and without the panopticonic gaze of a Regulator, evictions in England have been decreasing every year since 2013. In one year, eviction numbers fell from almost 6000 in 2013 to 4500 in 2014 (The Ministry of Housing, Communities and Local Government, 2019a). Scotland on the other hand, with all of its policy innovations, protections and legislative protections, has seen the numbers of evictions increase by an incredible 44% over the last five years (Shelter, 2019). The 'progressive' prescriptions of the *Housing (Scotland) Act 2010* had only a brief effect before the numbers returned to levels in place before the 2012 implementation date.

This places a radical doubt upon whether or not the issue of evictions for rent arrears can be managed through regulatory oversight, or resolved through legislative interventions. The issue, as we shall see when the evidence is presented in Case Studies 1 and 2, is about affordability, something we will return to in Parts II and III of this book.

Coda: The Limits of the Law

One of the most striking contradictions to emerge from this programme of legal and regulatory intervention in both the social and private housing sectors of the UK, is represented by the impact of the *Immigration Acts of 2014 and 2016*[3] (evidence regarding this issue will be presented in Case Study 3 in Part II of this book). For the purposes of this chapter, it will suffice to say that after the great lengths that all three governments discussed above have gone to, to provide added protection against eviction, these have been systematically removed by Westminster in all cases concerning migrants who do not have leave to remain in the UK. As a central part of the Home Office's 'hostile environment for immigrants' policy, the punitive prescriptions of the *Immigration Acts 2014* and *2016* criminalise not only the status of the immigrant, but the conduct of anyone seen to be assisting them, including in the provision of housing. The *Immigration Act 2016* states that landlords who do not comply with the prescriptions laid out in the Right to Rent section can face up to five years in prison. The Immigration Acts also remove any requirement to follow the ancient protocol of issuing the correct notices and seeking a decree from the Sheriff Court. In short, the protections from summary eviction enshrined in housing law are overridden by the requirements of the Immigration Acts. Security of tenure, and protection from eviction are, it seems, entirely dependent upon 'status'.

At the time of writing, a group of law centres and housing law charities working together to fight against planned lock-changes of over 300 asylum seekers in Glasgow by the private firm Serco who were contracted to oversee the out-sourced provision of accommodation while applicants await their decision from the Home Office, has been lost. The group of legal actors took their appeal to the Court of Session in Scotland in November 2019, claiming that Serco's lock-change policy could breach the right to private, home and family life protected by *Article 8 of the European Convention on Human Rights* and the *Human Rights Act 1998*. This was rejected by the court who concluded that because Serco is not acting as a public authority in this context, it is not bound by human rights legal obligations in the same way a public authority would be. The group representing the asylum seekers have committed to taking this case to the UK's Supreme Court in 2020.

Notes

1 The concept of rentier capitalism will be dealt with in more detail in the next chapter. For now, it must suffice to say that rentier capitalists seek to monopolise physical, financial and intellectual property in order to maximise their profitability through rent. In opposition to industrial capitalists, rentier capitalists' profit without contributing to society.

2 The global financial collapse of 2008 was arguably the most serious financial crisis since the Great Depression of the 1930s. A toxic mixture of predatory subprime mortgage lending by banks, deregulation and overleveraging caused the collapse of Lehman Brothers Bank, the effects of which were felt throughout most of the world resulting in massive bank bailouts in all countries, with the exception of Iceland.

3 For more a more detailed account of the Immigration Act and its effects see Crawford, McKee and Leahy (2016), Leahy, McKee and Crawford (2018), Crawford, McKee and Leahy (2019), and Crawford, Leahy and McKee (2019).

References

Anderson I. and Serpa R. (2013) 'The right to settled accommodation for homeless people in Scotland: A triumph of rational policy-making?' *European Journal of Homelessness*, *7* (1): 13–41.

Citizen's Advice (2018) *Complain and You're Out: Research Confirms Link between Tenant Complaints and Revenge Eviction*. Press Release.

Crawford J., Leahy S. & McKee K. (2016) 'The Immigration Act and the 'Right to Rent': exploring governing tensions within and beyond the state'. *People, Place and Policy Online*, *10* (2): 114–125.

Crawford J., Leahy S. & McKee K. (2019) 'More than a hostile environment: Exploring the impact of the Right to Rent part of the Immigration Act 2016'. *Sociological Research Online*, https://doi.org/10.1177/1360780419867708.

Crawford J., McKee K. & Leahy S. (2019) 'The Right to Rent: Active resistance to evolving geographies of state regulation'. *International Journal of Urban and Regional Research*, https://doi.org/10.1111/1468-2427.12731.

House of Commons Library (2018) *The Use of Section 21 Evictions in the Private Rented Sector*, Number CDP-0258.

Hunter J. (2015) *Set Adrift Upon the World: The Sutherland Clearances*, Edinburgh: Birlinn Books Ltd.

Kemp P. (2004) *Private Renting in Transition*, Coventry: Chartered Institute of Housing.

Leahy S., McKee K. & Crawford J. (2018) 'Generating Confusion, Concern, and Precarity through the Right to Rent Scheme in Scotland'. *Antipode*, *50* (3): 604–620.

McKee K., Muir J. and Moore T. (2017) Housing policy in the UK: The importance of spatial nuance. *Housing Studies*, *32* (1): 60–72.

Ministry of Housing, Communities and Local Government (2019a) *Local Authority Housing Statistics: Year ending March 2018*, London: Ministry of Housing, Communities and Local Government.

Ministry of Housing, Communities and Local Government (2019b) *A New Deal for Renting: Resetting the Balance of Rights and Responsibilities between Landlords and Tenants – A Consultation*, London: Ministry of Housing, Communities and Local Government.

Scottish Housing Regulator (2016) Landlords' performance against the Scottish Local Housing Charter 2013–2016, www.housingregulator.gov.scot/.

Shelter (2009) *Implementing Section 11 of the Homelessness Etcetera (Scotland) Act 2003*, Shelter Policy Library.

Shelter (2012) *Evictions by Social Landlords in Scotland 2010–11*, Shelter Policy Library.

Shelter (2014) Shelter exposes true scale of 'revenge evictions'. News item: www.shelter.org.uk updated 25 March 2019.

Shelter (2017) Eviction from a private tenancy accounts for 78% of the rise in homelessness since 2011. Press release: www.shelter.org.uk.

Shelter (2019) *Evictions by Social Landlords in Scotland 2016–2018*, Shelter Policy Library.

Stalker A. (2007) *Evictions in Scotland*, Edinburgh: Avizandum Publishing Ltd.

3 A Political Economy of Housing in the UK

Exposition

Having widened the lens in order to capture the legal world within which evictions are regulated and governed, this chapter will open the aperture further, in order to relate the issue of evictions to the historical development of the political economy and its effects on the housing sector in the UK. The archaeological character of the process of historicisation will unearth three important points, each addressed here in turn. With the historical development of capital accumulation, and its transformation from industrial to finance capital and then into the universal proliferation of rentier capitalism that we see today, this chapter's relevance expands beyond the coastal boundaries of the Island of Britain, to encompass most of the modern world.

By way of an exposition, the three points that this historicisation unearths, are as follows:

1. There is a strong correlation between the type of housing provision and the economic system of any given epoch. The five distinct 'generations' or 'cohorts' (in a Mannheimian sense) that have developed over the last century, are all closely connected to the political economy that was dominant at that particular time. This conceptualisation firmly rejects the notion of the 'invisible hand of the market', bringing the state centre stage, to uncover the effect of the 'invisible hand of the powerful'.

2. The current notion of a 'housing crisis' is, from a realist perspective, deeply misplaced. If there are severe housing shortages and massive levels of housing inequality in every single major city in the world, it is not because the housing systems are defective or faulty, but exactly the opposite; this is how the system 'actually' works. This is how it was designed to work by those who benefit from it most. The global 'housing system' works effectively as a means of surplus value extraction through the generation of a real estate market and, most significantly, through rent. The current housing situation is only 'in crisis' from the perspective

of those who rely on the *use value* of housing to provide somewhere decent to live and reproduce their lives in relative comfort.

3. If, as suggested here, the housing system is 'dysfunctional', then it must be accepted that the notion of the housing 'crisis' and the 'housing market' are one and the same thing, mistakenly split into two different entities. From the 'crisis' perspective, which regards the housing systems around the world as being inadequate as a result of their almost universal inability to provide decent affordable housing for all, it must also be accepted that this self-same crisis will never be solved with market-based solutions. If people around the world are to enjoy better and more affordable housing conditions, a radically different model is required, one that engages with the problems experienced by both volatile and unpredictable markets on the one hand and the 'planned' failures of centralised urban development, as for example, in the former soviet states on the other.

Development

Following on from the exposition above, this section will expand and develop these three theses in turn.

> There is a strong correlation between the type of housing provision and the economic system of any given epoch.

The historicisation of the relationship between the political economy and the dominant form of housing at any particular period, uncovers the fact that for certain sections of the population, the housing options available to them have rarely been a matter of choice. Rather, they have been overdetermined by the very specific needs of the form of capital accumulation that has been dominant at that particular time. This assertion will be evidenced by taking each cohort in turn, in an attempt to show the extent to which there is a strong correlation between the main form of housing tenure and the dominant means of wealth accumulation in any particular period.

Cohort 1 – The Industrial Slum-Dweller

The British industrial revolution had a profound impact on the political economy, not only that of the UK, but arguably the entire world. With the development of heavy industry and the technical innovations which flourished, the population of Britain's towns and cities exploded and living conditions quickly became squalid. Throughout the 19th century, there was added pressure from the Highland clearances, where entire populations in the north of Scotland were removed from their land in order to make way for sheep (Devine, 2019). Those who remained in Scotland moved to the towns and cities, looking for work, adding to the overcrowding conditions. There were several waves of Irish immigration due to a combination of famine and eviction, and cities like Liverpool, Manchester and Birmingham (as well as Glasgow, Dundee and Edinburgh) benefitted from their cheap labour and ability to cope with severe conditions of hardship (Engels, 2009 [1845]).

By the middle of the 19th century, there were concerns about public health and its effects on both the reproduction of labour and Britain's ability to recruit an army fit for purpose in an age of Imperial expansion. These bourgeois anxieties resulted in a shift from the laissez fair attitude that led to overcrowding in slum tenements to the beginnings of state intervention with the *Royal Commission on the Housing of the Working Class in 1884*. This resulted in the *Housing of the Working Classes Act 1885* which took the first steps towards the levels of state intervention that were to follow in the century to come.

The British state's intervention into housing conditions in the UK's major industrial centres, benefitted employers by improving the general health and productivity of workers, but the push for reform was not entirely top-down. Growing levels of worker militancy and trade union organisation also played their part. Worker populations within cities such as Glasgow were instrumental in driving progressive change through housing reforms and state intervention. At its height at the end of the 19th century, Greater Glasgow had almost one million inhabitants, double its' current population, giving it the status of being 'the Second City of the Empire', second only to London.

The explosive combination of a powerful and organised cartel of private landlords on the one hand and a militant tenant population on the other, lead to the inevitable clashes that would result in some of the most radical state interventions to date. Many of the most active of the tenant organisers were the children of families who had been forcefully removed from their homes in the Scottish Highlands as well as the Irish who had been evicted from their farms or who had fled starvation at a time when British absentee landlords were exporting record levels of crops out of Ireland. What emerged from the atrocities, massacres and mass evictions on certain sections of the population by the British landed classes, was a highly politicised and well-organised group of activists who were already predisposed in their antipathy towards the rentier class who continued to exploit them.

World War One brought the munitions industry to Glasgow, with some 20,000 workers employed in maintaining Britain's war effort, adding pressure to a privately rented tenement housing stock that was already creaking under the weight of overcrowding. With a large percentage of the male population in the trenches, much of the vital munitions work was done by women. Taking advantage of what they thought was a weakened tenant cohort, the cartel of private landlords in Glasgow began to raise rents to unaffordable levels. What the private landlords had not bargained for was a well organised and resolute tenant population on one hand and a British government that had an interest in keeping the costs of the war under control on the other. Spiralling rents meant higher wages, a factor that would result in increased costs in an armaments industry that was itself entirely privatised.

As the cartel of private landlords began eviction proceedings, the women of Glasgow defended themselves rigorously, and robustly. Great leaders emerged, many of whom had experience of organising direct action as Suffragettes, with some of the women being active Communists in the Red Clydeside movement. This political experience allowed them to collectively resist, with physical force, the repeated attempts of Sheriff Officers in carrying out the evictions. Mary Barbour from Govan and Helen Crawfurd from the Gorbals, were among those who lead the famous Glasgow Rent Strikes of October 1915. Some 200,000 tenants, mostly women took to the streets and made clear their intention to pay only the rent stated in their tenancy agreements (Taudevin, 2015). By 25 November 1915, the Westminster Parliament had passed the *Rents and Mortgage Interest (War Restrictions) Bill* and by 25 December it had received Royal Assent. Although most workers still lived in private rented accommodation that consisted mainly of overcrowded tenements in insanitary conditions, rent controls were now in place across the UK.

Cohort 2 – Generation Social Rent

The end of World War One saw the implementation of the *Housing, Town Planning, &c. Act 1919* (sic) also known as the *Addison Act*, with plans for local authorities to build some 500,000 'homes for heroes'. The financial difficulties of the 1920's depression meant this number was reduced by half, but it still represented a landmark moment in the development of working-class housing. Social housing, however did not really replace the private rented sector until after World War Two, when it became the dominant tenure in the UK. There is no doubt that the election of the Labour party, the work of John Wheatly and the rise of the trade union movement played a significant part. However, the Conservative party actually oversaw the most ambitious building programme in its plans, under Harold Macmillan in the 1950s, to build houses for the *least well-off* workers (at a time of near full employment).

As the political economy moved from heavy industry to a Fordist-Keynesian model after World War Two, the private rented housing sector was deemed to be an insufficient means to reproduce the necessary labour force, one that was healthy and well educated enough to produce the efficiencies that modern industry demanded. For British industry to remain competitive at a time of rapid development from other countries around the globe, particularly those that were winning their independence from British Imperial rule, it required significant subsidy from the state. An adequate supply of affordable social housing was one such means of suppressing wage rises at a time when *worker-power* was at its strongest.

Thus, to a large extent, social housing was to the Fordist-Keynesian period what rent controls were to the industrial-war period. They both arose from the dialectical relation between the requirements of the dominant form of political economy on one hand and the pressures of organised labour on the other. Rent controls benefitted both munitions workers and the state's war effort simultaneously. The collateral damage in this struggle were the landlords. Parliament's swift move to restrict rent increases was evidence that the economic interests of landlords were simply discordant with those of the state, and threatened the war effort. That is not to say that the militancy of the women who took direct action was not instrumental in securing the legislative measures required to curb runaway rent increases. But the timeous nature of the government's response is a clear indication that it was also very much in their interests to curtail the power of rentier classes at that particular time.

Social housing was a great boon to the workers of Great Britain, but it must not be forgotten that it was also a direct state subsidy for industrial capital. As long as this type of industrial production was a dominant feature of the British economy, then social housing would be the dominant tenure.

Cohort 3 – Generation Lucky Buyer

The dismantling of the Fordist-Keynesian compact was accompanied by the destruction of the municipal dream. The utopian visions of the Garden City Movement and the ultra-modern plans of Le Corbusier's vertical villages of hyper-utility were torn asunder and a new future in which Margaret Thatcher's vision of a homeowning-democracy was quickly normalized and adopted wholesale. The 'Big-Bang' de-regulation Conservative Government under the leadership of Margaret Thatcher wasted no time in revolutionizing finance in the 1980s, as well as 're-regulating' the ability of financiers to not only invest abroad for the first time, but to take on the role of both agent and trader, creating the contemporary role of 'stock broker'.

The implications for housing were almost as revolutionary as they were for the UK political economy. When industrial capital was displaced by the interests of finance capital, then not only was 'affordable' housing rendered obsolete, a need for unaffordable housing took its place. In other words, if industry relied on affordable social housing to suppress wage rises, the banks and building societies needed housing that was not only privatised, but that would continue to increase in value, driving up the unit cost of housing, thus augmenting the value of loans in the form of mortgages.

The 1980s saw a raft of state measures designed to achieve these objectives. Firstly, the Right-to-Buy your council house, a policy that arguably played a significant part in the election of the Conservatives in 1979, represented the single largest privatisation in UK history. Not only did it create a new group of homeowners by extending homeownership to former council tenants, the generous subsidies at which these homes were purchased made it economically damaging for councils to build more social housing, as they would be doing so at a considerable loss. Indeed, in Scotland, 50 years later, the Right-to-Buy was recently rescinded, along with a modest new wave of social housing built for the first time since the Conservative Government led by Margaret Thatcher allowed tenants to purchase their homes at knock down prices.

As the economic priorities shifted from production to finance, so too did housing tenure as homeownership overtook social housing, leaving private renting as a minority housing option. Again, this sea change within the political economy benefits the dominant economic and political class at the expense of the old guard of industrialists and manufacturers. At the same time, a section of the working classes was able to purchase what would become a highly valued asset at a very generous subsidy[1]. Add to this mortgage deregulation and a raft of financial incentives that created affordable house prices, and a generation of 'lucky buyers' emerged out of the ashes of the loose collectivism of social housing.

Cohort 4 – Generation Housing Bubble

The generation of lucky buyers were fortunate as the process of financialisation, when introduced in the UK, meant that house prices were relatively low. In a growth economy where money was created by banks through granting loans with interest, this would not last. When Tony Blair's Labour Party took office in 1997, contrary to expectation, the 'marketisation and commodification of everything' was ramped up beyond levels even the Conservatives had thought possible.

Continued mortgage deregulation and financial liberalisation gave lenders the freedom to expand the market to those who were previously excluded through a raft of lending mechanisms and financial instruments including 100% mortgages, interest-only mortgages and self-certification mortgages. Government backed initiatives also expanded the market to include those who had, thus far, been excluded from homeownership. These included 'help-to-buy' (in the form of a deposit as house prices doubled between 2002 and 2008 and 'shared ownership') a scheme that allowed households to purchase a share of a house from a social landlord who would own the remaining share. The UK followed the US and by the time households were regularly being given 125% mortgages for housing at vastly inflated prices, the bubble had eventually burst.

Cohort 5 – Generation Rent

Banks make money from interest on loans. In fact, this is how money is largely created in most economies, through the provision of loans paid back at interest. For an economic model that is based on compound growth the importance of finding an increasing stream of new customers is paramount. The banks, having exhausted the limits of credible loans, began extending these markets to more and more people who were less and less likely to be able to afford to pay them back. Add to this an entire industry based on taking kick-backs and fees at each stage of the process, an overcomplicated system of mortgage-backed securities and collateralised debt obligations under the unwatchful eye of a credit rating system that gave even the sickest products a clean bill of health, and serious problems were on their way. Once things began to unravel and no one in the investor community knew whether they held a good investment or a bad one, confidence collapsed and a credit crisis reverberated across the globe. Iceland jailed the bankers, refused to bail their institutions out creating instead their own national bank, and was back in good health within three short years. The rest of the world, however, took the bail out option, and most are still feeling the adverse effects over a decade later.

Not everyone lost out. The beneficiaries included those involved in various forms of disaster capitalism, such as hedge funds and those who were betting against the market. In very general terms the global banking collapse of 2008 had two broad effects; it made the very rich and powerful much richer and much more powerful while at the same time crushing the last vestiges of organised worker-resistance.

According to Forbes, the wealth of the world's billionaires rose from $2.5 trillion in 2009 to almost $9 trillion in 2019. In 2019 trade union membership grew slightly among the professions but remained in freefall for the lowest and most insecure sectors of employment. In the UK, less than a quarter of employees are trade union members (GOV.UK, 2018). One of the most significant developments was the growth of the 'gig economy' an entirely lopsided employment relation that introduced unprecedented levels of precarity to those at the margins of the social and economic sphere while guaranteeing significant shareholder dividends.

The UK Government's response to the 'crisis' was to introduce plans that entailed significant cuts to welfare and social services. Welfare conditionality was ramped up and benefit sanctions left families without welfare for anything between three months and three years. In 2019, Dr Philip Alston, the UN rapporteur on extreme poverty and human rights reported that the UK Government's policies had led to the systematic immiseration of millions across Great Britain. Fourteen million people were living in poverty in the fifth largest economy in the world, and by 2021, he predicted that a staggering 40% of children would be living in poverty (Alston, 2018). The game was up for compound growth in the mortgage market. They had been scraping the empty barrel for so long the bottom fell out.

We have, it seems, come full circle. The early part of the 21st century, just like that of the century before, is now defined by increasing levels of job precarity, declining standards of living, insufficient welfare provision, alarming levels of poverty and deprivation and of course the return of the rentier capitalist. This leads to the second of our archeological finds, the one that asserts that the notion of a housing crisis only makes sense from the perspective of those who use housing as a means of shelter, and how for those who profit from rent and real estate speculation, the housing system has never been more effective and efficient (Jacobs 2019).

> 2. Housing is in crisis only for those who prioritise its use value. For those who prioritise its exchange value, it has never been a more effective and efficient system.

This is one of the central points made in Madden and Marcuse's book *In Defense of Housing* (2016). It is founded upon the argument that housing has two distinct forms of value: use value and exchange value. This development of Marxian thought holds that since the period when Sapiens made the transition from the Mesolithic (hunter gatherer phase) to the Neolithic (farming phase) around 12,000 years ago, human beings have had to concern themselves with the search for somewhere to live. The First Disruption, as Bastani (2019) calls it, came after millennia of nomadic existence, a period when the human connection to nature was at its most profound, and resulted in Sapiens, for reasons known only to themselves, hanging up their spears and taking up tools (Harari, 2011). This was the most significant change to date, to both the lives of humans and their environment and things would never be the same again. Farms were established and dwellings of a sort were built. Since the First Disruption, housing has had a very strong use function; as shelter, somewhere to rest safely and to reproduce and nurture the extended family. During these years housing has been tied to land and work and in feudal times, tied to the landowner and the system of patronage that it entailed. It was not until fairly recently that housing itself became a commodity, something from which profits could be made.

There are extreme housing shortages and problems of affordability in every single city in the world. The point Madden and Marcuse (2016) make is that to see this as 'a housing system that no longer works' is misplaced. For those who control the global housing market and, whom it benefits most, (i.e. the investors, the real estate developers and the rentier class), the housing system has never been more efficient nor more effective at generating surplus wealth.

The commodification of housing and real estate through the privileging of its exchange value over its use value means that it is working exactly the way it has been designed to work. This is clear, because it serves, with the greatest of efficiency, and with the utmost reward, those who have the greatest degree of influence over it. Global increases in the levels of homelessness, evictions and foreclosures are merely collateral damage in the war to extract as much profit as possible from housing and real estate markets around the world (Jacobs 2019).

The current economic system within which homelessness and forced removals are taking place is defined by the fact that global real estate is estimated to be worth at least $217 trillion (36 times more than all the gold that exists) and accounts for 60% of the entire world's capital (Stein 2019). Three quarters of this unfathomably large sum is in housing. Housing is therefore the dominant means of wealth accumulation in the world today. Add this to the influence of the structures of regulatory capitalism and the scene is set for a social housing system that prioritises rent over all other possible factors. As Stein points out, given the position of real estate as the dominant means of surplus wealth extraction in the global economy, it is not surprising that, at the time of writing, the President of the world's biggest economic superpower is himself, a real estate developer, as were his father and his grandfather.

To be able to say that there exists a global housing 'crisis' is to speak from the perspective of those who rely upon the 'use value' of housing, those who require housing as somewhere to live. From this perspective, housing is, for the vast majority of people living in global cities and major conurbations, either largely unaffordable, or mostly undesirable due its poor condition or unsuitable location. In order to assert the dysfunctionality of a housing system that benefits real estate investors and rentier capitalists, at the significant expense both socially and economically, of those who seek housing as a place to live, we must first of all bring into question the role of the 'market' as a means of distribution of access to accommodation, housing rights, rents and profits.

> 3. From the perspective that the housing system is dysfunctional, it must be accepted that the notion of the housing 'crisis' and the 'housing market' are not separate things, but *the same* thing.

In order to make the point that housing 'crisis' and housing 'market' are the same thing viewed from slightly different perspectives, it is imperative to firstly explore the extent to which the housing market, like all other markets, is almost entirely reliant upon the state for its creation, functioning and promotion.

The Myth of the Free Market

As Karl Polanyi first pointed out in *The Great Transformation* (1944: 194) there exists an enduring and seductive myth regarding the false notion of the 'free' market. It is seductive because it offers the (false) promise of a utopian vision that removes the requirement for a messy and conflictual politics replacing it with the natural order of self-interest (that benefits us all) and equilibrium. Deleuze and Guattari (1983[1972]) developed this idea in their own work, showing the extent to which capitalism was never liberal, it has always been state capitalism. Bourdieu (2005) *The Social*

Structures of the Economy, details the ways in which the state operates at every level of the so-called 'market'. From the creation and regulation of money (quantitative easing), the levying of taxes, the control of inflation, the suppression of interest rates, to the creation of markets through a wide range of incentives, policies and enticements, that serve to oil the wheels of both the production and consumption of housing. This accords with the above appraisal of the fact that when we historicise housing, we find that the dominant tenure is always that which best serves the dominant means of capital accumulation and surplus value extraction. This alignment would be impossible if it were not for the work of the state and its institutions. Out of one myth we can dissolve another, one that has for so long been the mantra of market fundamentalism (also known as neoliberalism) and that is the 'invisible hand of the market'.

We must return to the first part of this chapter and ask, who set up the *Royal Commission on the Housing of the Working Class* in 1884? Who was it that passed the *Housing of the Working Classes Act 1885*? The market? No, it was Parliament. Following the rent strikes in Glasgow, who was responsible for implementing the *Rents and Mortgage Interest (War Restrictions) Act* in 1915, the market? No, again it was Parliament. The Right-to-Buy your council house, Mortgage Interests Relief at Source, Help-to-Buy, Shared Ownership and Buy-to-Let were all actions of the state in order to create markets by expanding their reach to those who had previously been excluded. If it is true, as Polanyi suggests, that the state and its institutions are responsible for the creation and functioning of markets, then it is the 'invisible hand of the state', rather than that of the mythical free market. Better still, given the fact that the state is neither a monolithic structure, nor is it governed by a unitary 'elite' or ruling class, but rather it is a site of struggle between competing interests, and so it is more accurate to talk about the 'invisible hand of the powerful'.

The doxa obfuscating the intrinsic truth about capitalism was exposed, perhaps more than at any other time, when the global banking system collapsed in 2008. After centuries of covert activity in the creation and control of the conditions of capitalism, states around the world intervened in ways that were unprecedented in peacetime. They did so in two ways; firstly, they intervened to save the banks, the bankers and the entire banking system (which ultimately caused the crash) and secondly, the states of the world intervened to ensure that it was their own populations that paid both the political and economic costs of the first intervention (Lazzarato, 2015).

The other transformation to arise from the collapse and rescue of the global banking system was the relegation of mortgage debt as the dominant means of wealth accumulation in favour of rent. Just as the transition from industrial to finance capital saw affordable homes being replaced by unaffordable homes, and social housing was replaced by homeownership as the tenure of 'choice', the banking collapse of 2008 resulted in a global decline in homeownership and a sharp rise in renting, particularly in cities and urban areas. The situation is almost the same regardless of which global city one lives in. If you want an apartment of reasonable size in a desirable location, you either require much higher than average wealth or earn the level of wages that can pay the exorbitant rent. From London to Paris, New York to Hong Kong, city centre accommodation is, for all but the economic elite, becoming increasingly unaffordable and largely out of reach.

The Real Estate State

The hyper-commodification of housing has not only replaced the use value with the exchange value of housing and real estate, it has made the extraction of the surplus of this exchange value the dominant means of wealth accumulation in contemporary society. Samuel Stein's (2019) book *Capital City: Gentrification and the Real Estate State*, makes the valid claim that a significant part of the problem is that planners are integral to the state-driven process of hyper commodification of land and real estate. This complicity between town and city planning officials and real estate state arises from a set of well-meaning professional practices and collective conventions. Wedded to the mythologies that underpin 'free market capitalism', they see no alternative way to organize cities beyond the narrow economistic paradigms dictated by the requirements of compound growth and a steady increase in both asset values and rent.

Even for Stein, who comes himself from the planning community, planning is intrinsically linked to the expansion of capitalism. If it is claimed that the housing market and the housing crisis are the same thing, then the same can be said for surplus value extraction and gentrification. Because of the importance planners place upon raising land and property values through finding the 'optimum', the highest value use of the land, then planning practices invariably result in an exacerbation of the worst excesses of capitalism. It is the constant need for property value inflation to guarantee investment returns, shareholder dividends and most importantly high rents, that produces the ills that we associate with the notion of 'housing crisis'. Here we arrive at the crux of this third point, namely that the 'crisis' and the 'market' are the same thing, seen from slightly different perspectives.

Recapitulation

The very essence of the first point made in this chapter is simply this: the dominant form of the political economy, in any given epoch, determines the dominant form of housing. Put another way, the dominant tenure is a reflection of the dominant means of surplus value extraction. That is to say, tenure is the means by which housing is put to the service of capital accumulation. At the height of industrial production, social housing was the dominant tenure, providing both affordability for workers and a subsidy for industrial capital. When the industrial economy was replaced

Table 3.1 The housing market and the housing crisis

'The Market' *(the invisible hand of the state)*	*The Crisis* *(the effects of 'the Market')*
Distributes housing resources based on affordability	Increases homelessness through unaffordability – results in evictions and foreclosures. Reduces housing options and creates Generation Rent.
Encourages property development with the aim of augmenting value in real estate	Gentrification – gated communities of exclusion, displacement, housing inequality
Facilitates large-scale borrowing and props up failing banks, and dysfunctional economic models.	Debt-based economy – affordability (back to the top in a loop of never-ending cycles of inequality and exclusion)

by the debt economy, and financial institutions who provided loans made increasingly large profits from their repayments, home ownership rose to dominance. When the housing bubble burst, destroying the global banking system in 2008, and increased levels of accumulation by dispossession augmented the wealth of the global super-rich, 'rent' became the dominant means of surplus wealth extraction. In every city, in every county in the world today, private renting has been the tenure that has seen the largest growth. The return of the *rentier capitalist* completes what has been a one-hundred-year cycle in the political and economic development of global capitalism.

It is therefore, misleading to say that we are living through a 'housing crisis' that is one of the worst housing crises in a century. The reason being that from the perspective of those in whose interests the housing system is designed to work, it has never been more effective or efficient at delivering its objectives; namely, increasing levels of surplus wealth extraction. The notion of a crisis exists only for those who rely on the use value of housing, as somewhere to live and reproduce their lives. The only way to overturn this problem lies in a reversal of the prioritisations, replacing the privileging of exchange value with a renewed elevation of the use value of real estate. Capitalists might be inclined to say that to re-prioritise the function of housing and real estate would require levels of state intervention that are simply impossible within our current political economy. This of course would be a misguided claim, since the political economy is, and always has been, heavily dependent on the continued intervention of the state. This leads to the third and final point of this chapter.

Not only is the notion of the 'free market' a myth, so too is the notion that the state's intervention in the capitalist system, 'inhibits' its development, 'suppresses' its growth and 'hinders' its potential to be truly innovative in ways that would overcome the internal contradictions that have plagued it for centuries. The opposite of all of this is true. Markets are created, promoted and sustained by the state, through a complex and protracted period of de-regulation in some areas and re-regulation in others. This has facilitated the continued growth, not only in surplus value, but in levels of extreme inequality.

What this chapter has shown is that, as far as housing priorities are concerned, it really is about the political economy. This political economy, and its regulatory functions have resulted in the return to a form of *rentier capitalism* that exploits precarity and insecurity on the one hand (see Standing, 2016) and rising rents and gentrification on the other. It shows that the crisis exists for those who rely upon the use value of housing and that this crisis, when viewed from their perspective, is inseparable from the housing market. In short, the housing market and the housing crisis, are one and the same thing.

This excavation of the development of housing in the UK has been necessary to contextualise the legal and regulatory framework set out in Chapter Two. This widening of the aperture has facilitated an archeological investigation of the influential effect upon tenure of the political economy at any given epoch. The return of the rentier capitalist and the development of regulatory capitalism (see Raco, 2016) have not only been complimentary they have had a great deal of influence on the thinking that underpins the raft of legislative measures designed to tackle the standards of housing while largely leaving the regulation of rents and rental profits untouched. In the social housing sector, the obsession with managing rent, keeping arrears under control, and maximizing the landlord's rent collection potential, cannot be separated from the dominant form of wealth creation in the wider economy.

Note

1 It could also be argued that those who bought their home at a significant discount were enticed into a political trap in which they could no longer exercise their right to withdraw their labour in industrial action for fear of missing mortgage payments, and were brought into political alignment, against their wider class interests, with a property owning class with whom they shared little common interest.

References

Alston P. (2018) *Statement on Visit to the United Kingdom*, United Nations Special Rapporteur on Extreme Poverty and Human Rights, United Nations: Office of the High Commissioner.

Bastani A. (2019) *Fully Automated Luxury Communism: A Manifesto*, Verso: London.

Bourdieu P. (2005) *Social Structures of the Economy*, Cambridge: Polity.

Deleuze G. and Guattari F. (1983) [1972] *Anti-Oedipus. Capitalism and Schizophrenia*, Minnesota: University of Minnesota Press.

Devine T. (2019) *The Scottish Clearances. A History of the Dispossessed*, Milton Keynes: Penguin.
Engels F. (2009 [1845]) *The Conditions of the Working Class in England*, London: Penguin.
GOV.UK (2018) Trade Union Statistics 2018, www.gov.uk/government/statistics/trade-union-statistics-2018.
Harari Y. (2011) *Sapiens: A Brief History of Humankind*, Vintage: London.
Jacobs K. (2019) *Neoliberal Housing Policy: An International Perspective*, New York: Routledge.
Lazzarato M. (2015) *Governing by Debt*, Chicago: Semiotext(e).
Madden D. and Marcuse P. (2016) *In Defense of Housing*, London: Verso.
Polanyi K. (2002 [1944]) *The Great Transformation. The Political and Economic Origins of Our Time*, Boston: Beacon.
Raco M. (2016) *State-led Privatisation and the Demise of the Democratic State: Welfare Reform and Localism in an Era of Regulatory Capitalism*, London: Routledge.
Standing G. (2016) *The Precariat: The New Dangerous Class*, London: Bloomsbury.
Stein S. (2019) *Capital City: Gentrification and the Real Estate State*, London: Verso.
Taudevin J. (2015) *Mrs Barbour's Daughters (A Glasgow Rent Strikes Centenary Edition)*, London: Oberon Books.

Part II

The People of Housing

Introduction to Part II

This part of the book sets out original data from three empirical studies presented here as case-studies. Each case-study emerged from a different research project, each one of which I was involved in personally as the interviewer. Together the three case-studies give a valuable insight into evictions and eviction practices, as well as providing evidence for further academic analysis.

The first case study asked the question, 'why do social landlords evict their tenants?' The participants were housing professionals from local authority and housing association landlords. The interviews were over an hour in length and discussed the causes of rent arrears as well as some of the more technical aspects such as discretion and the lodging of minutes for recalling the eviction decree. Towards the end of each interview, alternatives to eviction were explored.

The second case study examined the relationship between housing professionals who had statutory obligations towards their tenants and third sector rights-workers who helped tenants enforce these obligations. The participants were drawn from a range of professional roles relating to housing and had connections to the issue of eviction, either as housing professionals working for landlords and their representative organisations, or third sector and charity workers, who interacted with or had some involvement with housing professionals.

The third case study focused on the Right to Rent Part of the *Immigration Acts of 2014* and *2016*. This project began at the Geography Department of the University of St Andrews with Dr Kim McKee (project lead) and Dr Sharon Leahy, and is now ongoing at the University of Stirling under Dr McKee's direction. The fieldwork involved both public and private sector landlords, immigration lawyers, third sector workers and activists from both Scotland and England, and focused on their views on the requirement to evict or deny tenants access to housing if they did not meet the requirements prescribed in UK immigration legislation.

4 'I Just Want Tenants Who Will Pay Their Rent on Time'

Introduction to Case Study 1: Evictions for Rent Arrears

The central question of this case-study was: 'why do social landlords evict their tenants?' Interviews were carried out with housing professionals to examine their opinions on why rent arrears accrued and about professional interventions to tackle the issues. The study explored the use of discretion in the eviction process, asking professionals about their experiences and practice in this area. Views on tenant action were sought and in particular, research participants were invited to share their views on the legal process that allowed tenants, usually with the assistance of a solicitor or welfare rights worker, to recall the decree for eviction and to return to court to agree a payment plan. Finally, the case study explores professional perspectives on alternatives to eviction.

Background to the Research

Case Study 1 involved 35 in-depth interviews with housing professionals in the social housing sector. Twenty of these participants worked for local authority landlords and 15 worked for housing associations. There were five interviewees, from four local authority landlords with a large geographical spread.

The 15 housing association professionals were from ten housing associations of varying sizes, ranging from a few hundred units of accommodation to tens of thousands in the large cities. Identities of research participants and their employers have been anonymised.

Most of the 35 interviews lasted longer than an hour, with many brought to a close after 90 minutes had passed. The data from 35 in-depth interviews was voluminous, so given space restrictions and in order to be as succinct as possible, it will be presented here in summary form in four sections, reflecting the themes of the interviews.

Causes of Rent Arrears

The question 'what, in your opinion, are the causes of rent arrears?' was asked at the very beginning of each interview. What is striking is that almost everyone

Table 4.1 Local authority interviewees

Local authority	*Interviewees*
Council 1 – City	Head of Housing
	District Housing Manager
	Performance Team Leader
	Housing Strategy Officer
	Housing Officer
Council 2 – Rural	Divisional Housing Manager
	Area Manager Housing Services
	Area Housing Manager Housing Services
	Housing Officer
	Housing Officer
Council 3 – City	Senior Officer Rent Policy and Performance
	Project Manager Rent Services Redesign
	Income Rents and Tenancy Manager
	Neighbourhood Housing and Regeneration Manager
Council 4 – Urban/Rural	Head of Service
	Solicitor
	Service Manager Tenants and Homelessness Services
	Area Housing Manager for the Arrears Team
	Housing Officer
	Housing Officer

Table 4.2 Housing association participants

Housing association	*Participants*
Director	4
Head of Housing	4
Housing Manager	4
Income Control Manager	2
Legal Officer	1

gave structural reasons, rather than individual or pathological reasons for the accrual of rent arrears. The minority of interviewees who did refer to individual reasons for rent arrears did so after generally giving structural causes, but going on to claim that there was always a small group of tenants who did not want to pay rent. The answers to this question, in order of frequency were as follows:

1 Issues with the benefit system
2 The current economic situation in the UK
3 Employment issues – job insecurity, precarity and the rise of the 'gig' economy.
4 Multiple debts
5 Cost of living increases
6 Rising rents (particularly in the housing association sector)

Being semi-structured, the interviews often covered broad areas that led interviewees on different paths, but mostly in the same direction. These 'brief diversions' developed into explanatory exercises where the housing professional would go into great detail about all the various mechanisms and techniques that they employed for maximising the tenant's income in circumstances that were extremely economically challenging. When asked about the causes of rent arrears, almost all participants mentioned structural factors. Then, it seemed, they felt compelled to explain the effects of the economic situation and to go into a great degree of detail on the multiple interventions as well as strategic approaches which landlord organisations had developed to deal with the increase in rent arrears. These interventions arose from more than just the social landlord's institutional policies and procedures, they represented a sophisticated network of agencies and a wide array of external organisations which provided money advice, advocacy and legal representation to tenants who were in arrears or at serious risk of becoming so. Interestingly, the main themes here were effective management, efficient interventions, prompt action, innovative services, investment and control, all of which were used, to some extent, in ways that justified the process of eviction and those who enact it.

> Yes, we have our own welfare rights officer. We also sign post people to Citizens' Advice Bureau [CAB], and money advice etc.... We visit within a fortnight of a missed rental payment, we'd probably letter them first, then do a visit. Then we just escalate the process according to our procedures, we do night visits, morning visits, Saturday visits, we try everything to get people to talk to us. Then we try and engage them with the Welfare Rights Officer [WRO], if there's problems with benefits or anything like that so we do try everything to engage but the biggest problem is that quite often people just don't want to engage with us until they get the letter saying you're being evicted next week, by which time it's too late.
>
> (Housing Association #2)

Another research participant highlighted the importance of welfare advice in the process of tenancy sustainment.

> Yes, we have a full time WRO funded by the tenant's rents who bring in £400,000 to £600,000 in extra income a year. We're moving to a situation where all housing officers and front-line staff will be able to give some kind of financial advice at a basic level.
>
> (Housing Association #11)

Early intervention strategies were also a feature of prevention work as well as tenancy sustainment.

> We have a money advice worker from the CAB who works from this office. Part of the function is pre-tenancy work where new tenants can

> be referred so we can get in early, get people used to paying their utilities, Council Tax, rent arrears and some debt, multiple debt.
>
> (Housing Association #9)

As well as referring to external agencies, some local authorities employed their own specialists to work with issues that could lead to rent arrears. Another research participant noted:

> A number of years ago we looked at how we could improve and what we could do around rent arrears and we recognised that people weren't getting quick access to some of those services, so we actually fund two specialist housing posts within that team, so there's a housing welfare rights officer and a housing debt advisor, and they deal with tenants and people at risk of homelessness due to rent arrears.
>
> (Local Authority #2)

Having worked previously for Shelter in Glasgow, I was aware that social landlords had adopted strategies in which they enlisted the assistance of external agencies, such as welfare rights officers and money advice workers. I had not realised that in the few years since taking up my academic post and by the time I had started the field work for this research, so much progress would have been made in setting up a comprehensive network of professional organisations to deal with issues of poverty. What did surprise me was the number of landlords who had employed their own welfare advisors and money advice teams in order to maximise the income of their tenants, thus increasing their chances of paying rent. The interviewees were almost unanimous in their assessment that rent arrears were caused by a toxic combination of an entirely inadequate benefit system on one hand and a highly unfavourable economic system on the other. Only a very small number of interviewees mentioned individual failings at this stage.

Discretion

The question of discretion was put to the interviewees. The interviewees were asked, 'do you treat families and single person households the same throughout the eviction process, or is there a level of discretion involved?' Roughly one third claimed that they operated a discretionary system, one third said they often operated a system with some degree of discretion, and the remaining third of respondents claimed that they treated all rent arrears cases the same, irrespective of circumstances.

Landlords Who Use Discretion

Some interviewees from local authorities were aware of the divergent legal requirements between councils and housing associations. Some were also aware of the extra costs that these statutory obligations bring to councils.

> Aye, but then, I mean, they [Housing Associations] don't have the same responsibilities that we do to re-house homeless people and all that kind of thing, they don't necessarily need to have a social conscience in the way that a local authority does, and also the expense, the huge expense of re-letting a property, the cost of a re-let, the cost of putting the damage right, you know, some of them you don't have to have temporary accommodation but when there is temporary accommodation that's another expense as well, so I think various studies have worked out something between £17,000 and £25,000 a throw to re-let a house.
>
> (Local Authority #5)

One interviewee referred to the effectiveness of the legislative measures and guidance documents in shaping practice, particularly when applying discretion to evictions cases.

> As a council you have the seven pre-action requirements to meet, but with our early intervention protocols it's all about finding out what the personal circumstances are and it's based on that. So, if the tenants are vulnerable or need further support and things like that, you would hold off considering lodging that case for a decree, right, and you would try to get support in place.
>
> (Local Authority #28)

A common theme to emerge from the data, was that local authorities were more inclined to talk of *tenants* in a community sense (where tenants are known to them personally) and housing association staff to talk about 'customers' of whom they knew little:

> We deal with our cases from very small arrears right up, the housing officer continues the process right through so it means you know your tenant, you know what their circumstances are, you know what the background to the case is, so all of that would be taken into consideration before we take court action.
>
> (Local Authority #15)

Landlords Who Don't Use Discretion

> I would like to think that we treat absolutely everyone the same, everybody equally, irrespective of their circumstances.
>
> (Housing Association #6)

The interview data from the two local authorities mentioned above suggest that the cost of an eviction when re-accommodation is required is a major factor of consideration during the process. Households with dependent children will almost always have a statutory right to accommodation even if the tenant was evicted for rent arrears. This is significant as it is less relevant to housing associations than it is to local authorities who have the continued duty to accommodate households with children. This, it can be argued, is one of the reasons why the 2010 Act introduced the pre-action requirements (PARs), a legislative intervention that seems to have passed unnoticed in some housing associations:

> The fact that someone has a kid, I don't think is a major factor. Does the single tenant not deserve security any more than a family with children? You're aware of the consequences with children, we don't take the process lightly. Some housing associations absolve themselves from blame by passing responsibility over to the courts. That's not what we're about.
>
> (Housing Association #12)

This next interviewee confirms the last point given above:

> No difference, the same procedures apply. If they don't pay rent, then that person needs to lose their home, don't they? The sheriff would ultimately decide. But we wouldn't treat them any differently.
>
> (Housing Association #5)

The following participant did not mention the Pre-Action Requirements, and from their response, it seems that they may have forgotten about their imminent arrival. They were certainly not one of the landlords who had opted for early voluntary implementation:

> I will never ask what age the customer is, whether they have children or not, whether they have vulnerabilities, etc. I would expect that the services of the staff would have met whatever needs that household have. So, I suppose that the needs, in our opinion of a young person, an elderly person, a family, a lone parent whatever, can be met by us, so when it comes to the decision to evict, I look at the case in a clinical way, rather than ask about the circumstances.
>
> (Housing Association #2)

Landlords Who Sometimes Use Discretion

The two categories above provided some very unambiguous statements around the uses of discretion with housing associations being much less likely to be concerned with the household's circumstances than local authorities were. The data placed in the category 'sometimes uses discretion' was less specific. The examples below come from the category 'sometimes uses discretion':

> The fact is that we should no longer be treating everybody the same, and it's not done from the point of view 'oh that's a single man, let's make an example of him then because we don't have to re-house him as homeless or anything like that' but we always have these competing instructions. I suppose given from the Scottish Housing Regulator, they say you've to treat everybody the same and put procedures in place and all the rest of it, but then they will come back with criticisms that say 'you've given that person too many chances or whatever in comparison to somebody with kids' and all this kind'a thing.
>
> (Local Authority #3)

The next example highlights the conflicting demands of external agencies, in this case referring directly to the Scottish Housing Regulator:

> I've always felt that a lot of the housing associations in [....] operate probably more on a business-driven model in some senses, but even there I think some of the associations in [....] we certainly had much more co-operation with them in terms of re-housing homeless households etc... But I think probably the main difference is that as a local authority we have the statutory responsibility to deal with homelessness. If we evict somebody and we haven't considered all those household circumstances, they're going to go back through the revolving door.
>
> (Local Authority #7)

Minutes for Recall of the Decree for Eviction

A minute for recall is a legal remedy, actionable only once, where a tenant can recall the decree, through the Sheriff Court from which it was issued, in order to take the case back to court to come to a payment arrangement. By far the most common 'reason' for the recall being granted was that the tenant did not appear in person in court or was not represented in court, when the decree was granted. Unlike the issue of discretion, the division between landlords was not clear-cut. This issue was very much overdetermined by whether or not the landlord was a housing association which had no statutory duty towards homeless people, or a local authority that had.

The question surrounding 'tenant action' to stop the decree, mostly if not exclusively in the form of lodging a minute for recall, depended upon a range of factors, including firstly, whether or not the research participant thought they were effective in recovering the rent owed. This tended to be largely a subjective position, which very much depended upon personal experience of managing cases where recalls had been lodged. If their experiences were positive, they tended to be in favour and vice versa, irrespective of whether they were a local authority or a housing association. As we shall see, unlike the issue of discretion, the view taken on minutes for recall tended to be influenced by the extent to which they were used 'strategically' by the landlord, or whether the process was seen as something that simply prolonged the inevitable eviction.

Minutes for Recall Work

The responses would suggest that the interviewees who looked favourably upon minutes for recall viewed the process as being integral to the overall system of rent collection. Indeed, of the six landlords who said that they thought that recalls 'worked', many spoke of actively referring, or advising tenants to seek advice and in some cases advocacy in order to stop the eviction, get the case back to court and open up channels for facilitating the payment of the arrears. For these landlords, the process of tenant action was a welcome one, as it provided a dual benefit in assisting in the recovery of rent and having the potential to promote tenancy sustainment:

> I think they're useful. Last year we almost tripled the number of notices of proceedings we issued, which tells you something about our different tenant base. We got a number of units transferred from the Glasgow Housing Association [GHA][1]... of those 130 Notice Of Proceedings [NOP], 45 ended up with court actions being initiated.... We've actually walked some tenants straight in to [the law centre who are based in the housing association's building] (laughs) 'here's someone who can help and give you some advice ...' I just want tenants who will behave themselves and pay their rent on time.
>
> (Housing Association #12)

As with the section above on 'discretion' this research participant above alludes to the practice of landlords using local law centres in their attempts to get tenants to make payment arrangements. In this particular case, the housing association leased office space in their own premises to a high-profile community law centre which dealt exclusively in social welfare law. This would suggest that there was more to the arrangement than was perhaps being made explicit, with a tacit recognition that both organisations can benefit from their physical proximity.

> I don't think they're a waste of time, but I know from experience that tenants tend to put their heads in the sand. The minute for recall will give them another chance. Then, they realise that it is serious and they will deal with it. The court process is good at getting people to deal with the issue head on. It works, that's the thing. It prompts tenants to realise how serious it is. Once it actually goes to court, people wake up to the reality.
>
> (Housing Association #15)

This discourse revolves around the notion that the decree acts as an effective means of getting tenants to take the issue of rent arrears seriously. From the interviews, it seemed that housing professionals largely interpreted the low turnout at court hearings, as evidence that most tenants put their head in the sand. In the tenant's defence, the Sheriff Court is an intimidating place for anyone. In my experience as a Housing Aid Worker, tenants with multiple debts do not bury their heads in the sand deliberately, they are simply overwhelmed by the multiple debts they face. This causes them to be less than enthusiastic when another communication falls through their letter-box, informing them of the magnitude of their economic problems:

> A minute for recall is there, because nine times out of ten when we get decree, the tenant isn't there. But that's not our fault, we've done visits and letters. So, it's a legal technicality, I've never opposed a minute for recall. What I always ask for is a continuance. [Local community law centre] is really good at laying it on the line for the tenant. You're getting a continuation here, you need to stick to your payment plan, you only get one bite at the cherry here, you won't get another chance.... But no, not a problem with minutes for recall, they're there for a reason.
>
> (Housing Association #3)

This is an important insight as the court rules oblige Sheriffs to grant decree if the tenant or a representative does not turn up to offer a defence. The second issue is the recognition of the Legal Advocate as an 'ally' in getting the tenant to pay their rent arrears. The process of lodging minutes for recall was acceptable to the interviewee as the role of the Advocate was seen as having a doubly beneficial function.

Minutes for Recall Do Not Work

In contrast to the previous section where recalls were seen as being a fundamental part of the arrears management process, those who said they did not work, did so mainly on the grounds that they were an ineffective means of securing the payment of rent arrears. The issue of the tenants' right to be represented, and the other legal aspects of the court rules which govern minutes for recall were largely absent from the interviewee's statements in this section.

> Frustrated sometimes, yes. You kind of feel sometimes that sheriffs don't realize that the only money housing associations have coming in is rent money. They really don't appreciate that, and I keep saying that to solicitors, they've got to realize, it's all very well.... I mean minute for recalls are fine... some of them have worked most of them haven't, it's just a stalling tactic.
>
> (Housing Association #2)

It is important to note that after the eviction of a tenant, the only means by which the landlord can reasonably be expected to get the rent owed to them is to employ the services of a debt collection agency. After the eviction, the tenant moves on and rent owed becomes a former tenant arrear which has to, in effect, be written off. The issue here is that the minute for recall is seen as something which simply prolongs the process costing the association money, as these interviewees are of the opinion that very few of them result in payments being made. The next two examples provided by respondents mirror this sentiment:

> An absolute farce. I'll give you a live case – [explains an eviction with an arrear of £3,500 which was apparently unheard of in this area]. We'd invested a lot of time but we just got to the end of the road. We got decree and she got it recalled at the last minute. This is a very long process as you'll know. The recalling of the decree cost us over £1,000. She was working out of two jobs.
>
> (Housing Association #4)

> You're not doing the tenant any favours by letting the debt mount up. You need to close it down, we had one where a single parent woman ran up over £5000, that's not doing anyone any favours. This woman ended up in a private let and we lost the entire amount. When I worked for the council we used to hold it over tenants for up to six months, but that's not how it's done in housing associations. When I came here I realised that we act on decrees much quicker, we really should be executing it just after it's been granted really.
>
> (Local Authority #2)

During the field-work stage of this project, I noticed a general tendency for research participants to take a particular case (usually an extreme case) and talk about it as if it was somehow representative of the majority of cases they had. As was apparent, the individual cases with very high levels of arrears were used to illustrate the point. This respondent (#2 above) also alluded to the practice in councils where they 'hold decrees over tenants' for the maximum time period as a tactic for extracting rent owed. This response would suggest that if decrees could more readily be used as an effective tool for the extraction of rent, then they would be of much more use to the landlord.

The next excerpt is a clear example of a housing professional taking a very robust oppositional position against the mechanism:

> Personally, I detest them. The reason I detest them is ... we bend over backwards and force our staff to jump through a lot of hoops, before they go to court. We had one yesterday where the person has submitted a minute for recall, where they are claiming that they were unaware of

> what was happening. We've got notes on the account which say that we've had conversations with this person in the build-up. Confirmation that the letter had been received from our solicitor, nothing we can do, the recall must go ahead. I'm yet to see a minute for recall where I've been glad that it's been done. We understand why they are there. But when I look at – pre action requirements, the hoops are bigger and greater in number. I was a homeless officer in a previous role so I've seen it from the other side.
>
> (Housing Association #5)

Minutes for Recall Sometimes Work

A section of the housing professionals interviewed were not entirely convinced that minutes for recall always resulted in the arrears being recovered:

> We actually encourage people to go for them, particularly if there's a chance that we can actually get the money. We take every chance on recovering the rent owed. Frustrating at times, but that's what we do. We do object to legal aid. (Laughs) we don't think that in a Sheriff Court, a summary cause action, which is ultimately a civil action, we don't think that people need lawyers. We think people should get legal aid in order to fight legitimate action.
>
> (Housing Association #3)

The main issue here was the recovery of the money, a priority which seemed to be the biggest factor driving the entire process. The next participant saw the process as being of disproportionate benefit to the tenant. It was also seen as a mechanism whereby a very small number of tenants cost the landlord a considerable amount of money.

> They work in the tenant's interest. They're frustrating for us as we've done all the grunt work in order to get the case this far through the court process. They can now recall right up until the eviction, so they work to protect the tenants, give them another shot. But they drag out the process for us. But sometimes we can save the tenancy but you think, 'why didn't she just come to the original hearing, why didn't she engage?' And there could have been a few months less arrears on that account. But they do protect tenants. We have a wee core of people who will not do anything until you get to that stage. Which is really frustrating, as much as you say, we're here to help, please engage, people still bury their heads in the sand till it gets to decree being granted. That's frustrating from a housing officer's position, because you're back at the same doors. There's a wee core group. I mean it costs us a lot of money.
>
> (Housing Association #9)

This is a very insightful response as it combined two important aspects of the process of recalling decrees for eviction. First, in order to obtain a decree there was a requirement to demonstrate to the Sheriff that the tenant had been advised to seek advice, including the type of advice and advocacy which could result in a minute for recall being lodged. Second, that the process was often fruitless because the underlying causes of rent arrears (poverty and increasing joblessness), persist irrespective of the level of advice and advocacy.

Alternatives to Eviction

In light of the data presented from the previous three topics, this last section highlights the astonishing contradictions that emerged from the research, an incongruity that sits at the very heart of the paradox of evictions. The housing professionals, in answering the first question relating to the causes of rent arrears, almost universally provided structural factors, ranging from the inadequacy of the benefits system, to the erosion of job security and the growth in multiple indebtedness of social housing tenants, whom they identified as being the least affluent of all the tenure types. Given this almost universal commitment to structural, rather than individual causes of rent arrears, it is astonishing that in the last section of the interview, not one single housing professional interviewed thought there was any alternative to eviction. Two interviewees suggested downgrading the tenancy, and one of moving the household to another house in a less desirable area. This consensus is all the more remarkable when the fact that the 35 interviewees were taken from a wide range of occupational positions including housing officers, senior managers and directors, and from an even wider geographical spread is taken into consideration.

In these interviews, alternatives to eviction were unanimously and universally rejected as unworkable. In preparation for the research project, I had attended eviction hearings at a number of Sheriff Courts in Scotland. I was intrigued by the posters that adorned the corridors and clerk's offices of the courts. The central message of these posters was that non-payment of fines would result in a range of remedial measures, including, bank arrestment, wages arrestment and material confiscation such as car impounding. My logic seemed straight forward, if these remedial measures work for criminal fines, then they can work for civil law cases such as those rendered worthy of court action and potential eviction. Not so, it seems, and as will become apparent.

Short Scottish Secure Tenancy (SSST) as an Alternative to Eviction

The following two excerpts talked about downgrading the tenancy to a Short Scottish Secure Tenancy [SSST]. This is a variation on a technical legal process for dealing with 'nuisance neighbours', the aim of which is to manage anti-social behaviour through 'conditionality' (i.e. good behaviour will result in strong security of tenure, anti-social behaviour will result in precarious security of tenure, leading to possible eviction):

> So if you're a nuisance to your neighbours you can get a triple-S-T, but I'd say that if you don't pay your rent, then you are as much of a nuisance to your neighbours, because their future repairs, new kitchens, bathrooms etc are in jeopardy if you don't pay your rent.... I think there are alternatives in the grounds of down grading a tenancy, to a SSST.
>
> (Housing Association #9)

> I know a number of authorities where, if someone's got into rent arrears and they've reached that stage, they will do a sort of probationary tenancy, a SSST, and that's something that you could look at to sort of monitor whether or not they engage in the support.
>
> (Local Authority #1)

Moving the Household to a Less Desirable Area

What became evident throughout this section of the interviews was the elaborate frames through which housing professionals justified their own roles and actions as well as criticising the actions or inactions of others. These frames also appeared to create clear distinctions between deserving (those who can pay their rent on time) and undeserving (those who cannot pay their rent) tenants.

> I must admit I did think in the past that moving someone out of their three bedroom house with a front and back garden into something less desirable could've been an option, that you're not actually evicting them but you're actually taking away the family home and moving them out of that into something different, you know, cause what we found was... a few years ago where the majority of people who didn't pay were in the nicest areas, in the best houses with three bedrooms, upstairs/downstairs, main door houses, front and back garden and they weren't paying their rent. And then you had the poor young couple with a couple of kids living in a multi-story block, same size of flat as their house, paying their rent every single fortnight.
>
> (Local Authority #5)

This example above confuses preventing an eviction with preventing the homelessness that results. By removing a tenant from one house and placing them in a less desirable house in a lower-demand area, involves an eviction and one where, if the tenants refused to leave willingly would, like all other evictions, be carried out with force.

Bank/Wages Arrestments

When research participants flatly rejected the possibility of there being any alternative to eviction, the issue of the Sheriff Court posters was raised during the interviews. These posters, which adorned the walls of the court lobby and clerk's offices, contained information in the form of a warning that non-payment of court fines would result in wages arrested, bank accounts frozen, or cars impounded. Not one single interviewee was convinced that that this was a workable solution with regard to rent arrears, with the majority making the claim that tenants were not in the position financially to make this arrangement worthwhile.

For a few of the interviewees the issue was bank details, or gaining access to the tenant's bank account, either directly or via the employer.

> Yeah but if we don't have bank details or if somebody's not working, you know, the house at the end of the day is the only thing that we can really take, you know, we don't have anything that we can take off them.
>
> (Local Authority #5–4)

> No, people do not want to tell you their bank details, I could go and get a wages arrestment, which would be an alternative to putting someone out on the street. That's only as good as the bank account and on-going income coming in. We have previously initiated payment decrees with wage arrestment, but what generally happens is the person ends up being sacked because the employer doesn't like the fact that we're sniffing around, wanting access to wages accounts, etc.
>
> (Housing Association #12)

For a number of interviewees, the issue came down to inadequate income. The general consensus was that tenants who lived in council houses were mostly on some form of benefit, that a high level of wages would be required to facilitate either bank account or wage arrestment, and that in most cases the debt would continue to rise. There was also acknowledgement that high rents were, for many, unaffordable thus making the recovery process even more problematic. What is particularly interesting about the data in this section was the fact that it overlapped with much of the data contained in the previous sections, particularly the 'causes of rent arrears'. In both sections, the issue of whether or not the tenant actually had the money to pay rent was the central issue:

> Wage arrestments are an alternative but not many people around here have the kind of wages you can or want to arrest. We get direct payments etc., so we pursue that when we can.
>
> (Housing Association #13)

The next excerpt corresponds to the issue of part-time and insecure employment:

> The problem is, we have people on the margins, working part time, can't get enough hours, get tax credits etc. If I seize their wages then I'll get something, but the ongoing arrear continues. If anyone has any suggestions of alternatives then I'd love to hear them, but, as far as I'm concerned there are none.
>
> (Housing Association #14)

The issue of benefits was one of the most prevalent in the first findings section above:

> We have tried small claims in [....] before but it hasn't been very successful, but a lot of our tenants are on Benefit so it doesn't work for us very well. It's fine if you have a tenant who's in employment then obviously you can go down that route, but the majority of our tenants are actually on some form of Benefit, so it's not easy to administer that at all.
>
> (Local Authority #8)

The issue of high rents and the rising cost of living also featured frequently in the chapter on the causes of rent arrears:

> ... the problem that you've got with wage arrestments on the rent side of it is that the rent's so high now, you'd get something, but you're not getting it all ... you're always looking to reduce what the debt is they've got.
>
> (Local Authority #15)

A recurring theme appeared in this section, one built around a notion of having some kind of sanction to help with the enforcement of rental payments:

> Yeah but if we don't have bank details or if somebody's not working, you know, the house at the end of the day is the only thing that we can really take, you know, we don't have anything that we can take off them. I mean, personally, I probably shouldn't be saying this out loud but, you know, I think we need to look at things like giving people new kitchens and new bathrooms ... if someone owes you £2,000/£3,000/£4,000 why are you then going in and paying £5,000 to put a new bathroom in or a new kitchen, you know, you're saying to them 'you owe us this money but we'll still give you a kitchen and we'll still give you a bathroom and we'll still do X, Y and Z'.
>
> (Local Authority #5–4)

No Alternatives to Eviction

The interviewees were of the opinion that there was absolutely no alternative to eviction, although some wished that here was:

> I would love to, I would, I would love to be able to, you know, have an alternative that works, but again, really ... if we feel we've done everything that we possibly can and I think as a council we do, I think I probably do as much as I possibly can, and then at the end of that road if there's nothing more that can be done, I really don't know what the alternative would be?
>
> (Local Authority #4)

As with the answers to the question of the causes of rent arrears, the majority of interviewees invoked a mixed approach to justifying their evictions practice. This was, to a very large extent, viewed through a frame which focused on the efficacy and effectiveness of their own policies and procedures. The data suggested that the more comprehensive they considered their intervention and management strategies, the stronger the justification of their own actions as well as the stronger the criticism of tenants who did not pay rent. This produced a regime of justification and criticism which was almost circular and self-reinforcing:

> I think it is a combination of their circumstances, but I think we feel if we've done everything we can to try and prevent that eviction, at the end of the day if they're not going to engage, work with us and pay their rent then there isn't any alternative, and I think if you don't have that then other people would just see and then that has implications for the council's rental income,
>
> (Local Authority #15)

A number of housing professionals invoked their critical capacity against the non-paying tenant to such a degree that they almost completely exonerated themselves from any responsibility for the eviction action at every stage of the process. Blame is entirely shifted towards the tenant who did not pay. This is obviously contradictory, since many interviewees made it clear that in a large number of cases, structural factors and not indeed individual choices, were the main causes of rent arrears:

> In my opinion there is one alternative to eviction only and that's to pay your rent. We're in tough times as everybody knows, the fact that people that don't pay their rent is damaging their own neighbourhoods as much as if they were say, drug dealing or causing a nuisance, ... We never make a decision, to carry out an eviction the customer makes that decision for us. They will make that decision by definition of their

> actions. You know, it's never up to us what happens it's always up to them. Ultimately the decision is the customer's decision, do I want to keep my house, yes, then you need to talk to us, we will make an arrangement that is acceptable to us and affordable to them in a way that covers the middle ground.
>
> (Housing Association #9)

Some participants prioritised early interventions such as those mentioned when asked about the causes of rent arrears.

> Well, if there was any (alternative) surely some clever bugger before now would've found it, would be my off the cuff answer to you! The alternatives to eviction can only be tenancy sustainment measures like putting in tenancy support at an early stage, being more intensive about that, making sure that people's income is maximised through whatever means possible.
>
> (Local Authority #10)

As well as a means by which housing professionals shifted responsibility for the eviction from themselves to the tenant, the notion of the 'irresponsible' individual who jeopardised the collective interest of the community of tenants through the selfish act of refusal to meet their financial obligations, featured in a large number of interviews:

> I think the problem is the alternative to rent arrears debate ... alternatives to eviction debate turns around on we should never evict anybody for non-payment of rent. That's just not true, and nobody believes that. If somebody takes a property and wilfully refuses to pay their rent, everybody is clear the action is termination of that tenancy. Nobody would ever argue when you push them all the way through it that a non-evictions policy for rent arrears is in any sense reasonable, because you always run the risk of the individual who just says 'well in that case I'm going to help myself' so even the folk that would advocate a non-evictions policy don't believe in a non-evictions policy.
>
> (Local Authority #5)

The interviewee above evoked the notion of an almost contractual-like commitment between the landlord and the tenant which went beyond the position (taken by the majority of respondents) that the collection of the rent, however difficult to obtain, was the one thing that prevented the tenant from being evicted. The shift in terminology, from tenancy agreement to contractual relationship was accompanied by similar changes in how subjects and objects were framed, such as when tenants became customers and rent collection became income maximisation. The right-ward tilting of the field of social housing is accompanied by managerial tropes that promote the marketisation, commodification as well as individualisation of housing services. Not only does the contractualisation of their relationship shift 'responsibility' from landlord to tenant it also epitomises the essence of the privatised distribution of resources.

> It adds to the cost in what is a £16M/£16.5M revenue account, we probably commit a million/a million and a half, certainly a million pounds minimum to the effort of collecting the rent. And I don't mean processing the cash payments or running the direct debit system, I mean going out talking to folk who haven't paid their rent and trying to persuade them that they should pay their rent. A million pounds, at a substantial additional burden to other tenants, many of whom are on low incomes anyway, in order to get the rent in. Nine Housing Officers, four Income Max Officers, one Solicitor full time effectively on this, a Paralegal on this, you know, so ...
>
> (Local Authority #5)

Some interviewees were explicit that aspects of the process were about sending a 'message' to other tenants. This message had two facets, one that nonpayment of rent would result in eviction, and the other that in order to make tenants feel more reassured that their own efforts to pay rent were not in vain and that those who did not or could not pay rent were punished accordingly.

> There's an aspect of sending 'the message' out to other tenants that nonpayment will not be tolerated. We've been doing a lot of door knocking and maybe it's the Daily Mail attitudes but there are increasing numbers of tenants who would talk about their neighbours in terms of 'I'm going out to work and they're in there all day drinking, they don't have to work, both of us have to go out to work longer hours just to pay the rent', so there is a bit more prejudice. That's not always been the case, so they feel vindicated if one of their neighbours has been evicted for non-payment of rent.
>
> (Housing Association #3)

Recapitulation

This case study provides an invaluable insight into the personal views and opinions of housing professionals involved in evictions. The sample includes chief housing officers and housing association directors as well as senior managers, rent arrears managers and housing officers working at street-level. It is by mining the subjective aspects of housing practice that it is possible to gain insights that are unavailable to the objectivist or scholastic perspective. It is one thing to have a political or sociological overview of how housing practice relates to economic policy or the ways in which housing is influenced by the interventions of the state, but it is by taking seriously the subjective accounts of those on the inside that a much fuller picture of practice begins to emerge.

The interview data presented as evidence in this case study was, as one would expect, full of contradictions. At the beginning of each interview the participants were unanimous that the causes of rent arrears had a structural foundation, rather than resulting primarily from personal or behavioural factors. Yet, once the entire range of protocols, practices, pre-action requirements, interventions and procedures had been discussed, the housing professionals interviewed, held to the universal view that there were no viable alternatives to eviction. Although much of the discussion was framed, by the interviewees, around the collective conventions of the housing profession, what was interesting was the variation in answers relating to discretion and the tenant's ability to recall the eviction decree, taking the case back into court. The answers depended, not on the 'rigid' conventions of housing policy and practice but rather on the individual experiences of the housing professionals themselves. If they had experience of a specific intervention or 'approach' being successful, they tended to be more sympathetic. If, for example, their own experience of the intervention was that it was unsuccessful, then they tended to show opposition. Much of the evidence collected in this study suggests that a lot of professional practice is underpinned by financial and legal limitations and constraints, while some of it represents a more pragmatic approach, depending entirely upon the individual's views and experience.

Note

1 This transfer was through second stage stock transfer. The first stage involved 88,000 units of accommodation being transferred from Glasgow City Council to the Glasgow Housing Association (an RSL set up for this purpose). The plan was always that a second stage transfer would distribute these properties between existing RSLs.

5 'They Don't See the Bigger Picture'

Case Study 2: Relations Between Statutory and Voluntary Sectors

This, the second case study, explores the relations between the statutory housing sector that has obligations enshrined in law, and the voluntary sector that has a role in providing legal advice and advocacy. Understanding the relationship between these sectors is important for the wider purposes of understanding evictions. As the evidence contained in this chapter will show, the relations between third sector organisations that exist to 'enforce' the rights of tenants and the homeless, and those who are responsible for 'meeting' these rights, are often tense and confrontational.

It is significant that the first decade of the new millennium was a period of experimentation in welfare service provision with the notion of 'partnership working' playing a prominent role. Developed under the 'New Labour' government that took office in 1997, the concept of partnership working widely became the core vision for addressing organisational problems at institutional and local government levels. This involved a variety of co-working arrangements where diverse groups and organisations were required to collaborate in the interests of managerialist concepts such as 'service level improvement' and 'better outcomes' achieved with 'target driven', procedures through meeting a range of 'key performance indicators'.

This emphasis on 'partnership working', 'joined-up' approaches to service delivery as well as the co-production of knowledge for the purposes of policy development and better practice, meant that a number of previously unlikely alliances were struck between statutory and voluntary organisations. This was not implemented without resistance, indeed it was met with some hostility from both sectors. Front-line workers often saw the forging of partnerships as a compromise that served to dilute their ability to make the decisions they believed to be in the best interests of tenants and homeless people, at both an individual and collective level (Schmachtel, 2015). Most workers, however, simply got on with partnership working at a strategic level. An equal number were ultimately frustrated, for differing reasons, at the unforeseen difficulties of making these arrangements work (Manzi and Smith Bowers, 2004). At a managerial level, there was dismay at a lack of tangible results. On the frontline, there was concern over the endless tensions, animosities and conflicting priorities that emerged from working relations between different institutions (Wacquant, 2009).

For reasons that will be examined in more detail in Part III of this book, partnership working was never likely to be the silver bullet to cure the ills of a system that was underpinned by superficial short-term gains, rather than one based on quality and long-term objectives (Crawford, 2015). The different work cultures and divergent priorities created incompatible operational alliances, exacerbated by the external demands of 'regulatory capitalism' that set the institutions, agencies and groups at odds with each other from the outset (Raco, 2016). One of the added problems was that the impediments to having the same shared objectives were invisible to those who were trying so desperately to successfully deliver the 'joined-up' requirements needed to satisfy the politically driven 'what-works' agenda. In many cases, organisations that had contractual agreements to work together, to have training arrangements or strategic partnerships, simply reverted to the way they had traditionally operated (Holt and Kelly, 2018). Working practices oscillated between a disinterested superficial cordiality to a more tense and at times confrontational set of relations. The case study evidence presented in this chapter highlights the 'relational' difficulties that arise from a divergence of priorities, even when they arise between two institutions or agencies who claim to serve the interests of the same group, in this case, tenants and homeless people.

The Research

The case study emerged from a research project commissioned by a housing and homelessness organisation in the voluntary sector in the UK. For reasons of confidentiality, the organisation has been anonymized and is referred to here, and when referred to in the qualitative data, as the Organisation.

The qualitative study involved 30 in-depth, semi-structured interviews with senior staff members of relevant organisations across Scotland, the focus of which was to assess perceptions of the Organisation from partner agencies, stakeholders, competitors and those groups to whom it provided services of varying type. The research participants were chosen purposefully, rather than randomly, in order to achieve a good mix of key existing customers and potential customers. An initial contact list was provided by the Organisation. It included Heads of Housing in Scotland's 32 local authorities as well as a list of influential policy leads and contacts with which the funder had current or past service contracts. The list for this last group was informed by the Organisation who identified their main clients and customers, as well as their main competitors.

All of the research participants were selected because they held key positions, which included budgetary powers and the authority to enter into contractual arrangements with external organisations. Initial contact was made via a preliminary email which briefly outlined the objectives of the research as well as guaranteeing anonymity for the participants. These initial emails were followed up with telephone contact with dates set for face-to-face interviews or telephone interviews.

Reflections on Process

When I drew up the original list of interviewees, I was very well aware of who they were, due to their highly visible positions within the field of housing's main institutions. In my time at Shelter I dealt almost exclusively with housing professionals operating on the front line. Other than a few strategy meetings, and the occasional third stage homelessness appeal, I had no professional involvement with the very senior housing managers who made up the majority of the sample. Therefore, with the exception of a small number who were aware I had worked previously as a Housing Aid Worker, I was viewed as an academic.

Having drawn up a long list of potential research participants, with the key targets for interview at the top, I was surprised at the ease with which almost everyone agreed to participate. Very few declined, and those who did had good reason, mainly concerning their availability. Senior managers and directors of landlord organisations, lawyers, organisation workers, in fact, almost everyone I approached seemed very keen to have their say, to have their opinions considered regarding how they saw the commissioning Organisation and what they believed were its strengths and weaknesses, what it did well and what it could do better, or indeed, differently.

The Initial Responses

In response to questions concerning the Organisation's professionalism and reliability as a contract partner, the consultees were in unanimous agreement. Without exception, all of the interviewees held the view that the Organisation was very professional. Most took the position that the Organisation was easily the market leader in housing advice and campaigning. No interviewee who the Organisation had identified as a customer of stakeholder agency reported any previous or current problems working with them. Those with

Table 5.1 Participating organisations

Number of consultees	*Organisations participating in the research*
14	Local Authority (LA) Heads of Housing
5	National housing membership organisations
5	Third Sector organisations which have a connection with housing and homelessness
3	National funding bodies
3	Others (miscellaneous)

past or present contracts were satisfied that the Organisation had performed to a very high standard.

When asked about future contract possibilities, all interviewees said they would have no reservations about the Organisation being a reliable partner:

> They are a recognised brand which instills a great deal of trust in its advice and advocacy functions ... not quite 'the Post Office', but it's there or there about.
>
> (Local Authority Head of Housing)

Most of the respondents acknowledged the good work of the Organisation over the years, with many alluding to its campaigning role which has led to a raft of very progressive pieces of legislation affecting housing and homelessness:

> They have a lot to be proud of and can now more or less sit back and smoke cigars. Homelessness has been top of the agenda for the last ten years and an unprecedented amount of Acts which further their cause, and that of homeless and badly housed people, has been passed by the Scottish Government. All of these advances have been considerably influenced by them.
>
> (National Housing Membership Organisation)

There were, however, a number of contradictory positions that were coloured by two main criticisms. The first was the public 'naming and shaming' of authorities (an issue discussed below). This resonated across the sample, not only with local authorities, but more interestingly with most of the other interviewees. It related to what the respondents saw as the practice of drawing attention to a particular authority or landlord which the Organisation had deemed as failing to meet its statutory duties and obligations. The second arose from the opinions of local authority housing directors about the dichotomous position between the funder's national campaigning work (which was mostly seen as being of benefit to everyone, tenants and landlords both), and the individual casework and advocacy service which challenged landlord decisions on a case by case basis. Although this potential source of tension was widely recognized, the overall perception of the Organisation was positive; as one long serving senior member of an influential membership organisation pointed out, 'their lives would be easier without the Organisation, yet no one would like to see it go, such is its importance nationally'.

'Naming and Shaming': Criticisms of the Organisations' Propensity to Publicly Name Landlords for Bad Practice or Failing to Meet their Statutory Obligations

The broad consensus among research participants was that the Organisation's practice of naming and shaming served to alienate landlords and local authorities as well as key individuals. There was universal agreement on the fact that the practice of naming and shaming landlords who failed to meet their statutory obligations was counterproductive, and that it created unnecessary tension and in some cases animosity. It was suggested by the majority of interviewees that a more strategic approach, one whereby the Organisation worked more closely with authorities, would lead to better outcomes for both tenants and for those bodies responsible for providing their accommodation.

A number of local authority housing heads conveyed the fact that they thought the Organisation would do well to have a closer working relationship with the Association of Local Authority Chief Housing Officers (ALACHO), of which all of them were active members. Feedback from the interviews that supported the above included the following comments:

> Some councils are singled out when their figures appear bad yet often the baseline figures mask the truth about evictions. Often the worst authorities escape untarnished when authorities that have better track records for evictions are pilloried in public.
>
> (Local Authority Head of Housing)

The following excerpt, from a third sector homelessness organisation that provided similar services to the commissioning Organisation, highlighted the cultural differences in how they both went about their operational tasks:

> They have a different approach to us. We don't do naming and shaming. We don't think it is an effective way to achieve results.
>
> (Director of a National Homelessness Organisation)

The next example is from a local authority Chief Housing Officer, who wanted to see a better balance, more accurate statistical evidence, and a forewarning when they were about to be named in public as a landlord failing in their obligations:

> I have a lot of respect for the Organisation and the work that it does, but there needs to be a bit more balance to their approach, especially when condemning authorities and particularly when they use incorrect statistical evidence. Local authorities should be warned in advance when they are about to attack them, or their performance levels, in public.
>
> (Local Authority Head of Housing)

Concern about the Organisation's 'impetuous' approach was a recurrent theme in the interviews, particularly among landlord organisations:

> What compromises their 'image' is the fact that they are too quick to publicly condemn authorities without finding out all the facts. I hear a lot

> of organisations on the radio being critical of local authority practices. [another organisation] is the worst, but I've heard the Organisation take a pop at various authorities. I'm not always convinced that this type of criticism is productive.
>
> (Local Authority Head of Housing)

It was clear from the above examples that the practice of 'naming and shaming' in public was seen as being detrimental to the Organisation's position in a field in which it was seen as otherwise effective, commanding a great deal of respect.

'They Don't See the Bigger Picture': Perceptions of the Organisation's Rights-Based Approach

Another negative perception was firmly embedded in the advocacy function of the Organisation's housing advice service. This was not surprising given that organisations, and in particular those who lead them, do not like being challenged, notably when it involves court action or judicial review. This tells us as much about the power relations between landlords and their tenants as it does about the tensions between statutory and voluntary services.

One of the most illuminating contradictions existed in the gap between what housing professionals saw as their own areas of priority and what they perceived as the Organisation's role:

> For the Organisation and us to have a decent relationship we need to acknowledge we have different thresholds. The fact that on a daily basis I don't meet my statutory duties is something I'm quite used to, but it would not be appropriate for [the Organisation] to become used to that. There is a difficult balance to be struck here. I might not be able to do something about it. I prioritise x over y and they need to respect that. I sometimes have a problem with how they challenge, especially when they escalate the judicial review process.
>
> (Local Authority Head of Housing)

The candidness of many of the interviewees was, it could be argued, down to the fact that respondents were promised anonymity. Many talked openly about the fact that they saw the Organisation's priorities as being in some way different, and in some cases quite markedly different, from their own.

There was, in a few cases, a worrying trend which suggested that not all housing leads understood the full extent of their statutory obligations, an issue which might put them in more of a conflictual relationship than they might otherwise have been, had they had more 'insider' or expert knowledge of their field. There appeared to be a number of discrepancies between what certain heads of local authority housing services saw as their priorities and those the government had prioritised in statute. The vast majority of local authority Chief

Housing Officers talked about the fact that the Organisation, in pursuing its advocacy role, 'did not see the bigger picture':

> We recognise that we have very different roles.... Individual cases cause problems as the Organisation often doesn't see the bigger picture.
>
> (Local Authority Head of Housing)

The prevalence of this 'bigger picture' narrative is of significance:

> We recognise that there are different roles, but the Organisation only succeeds in pissing people off when it is being one-sided. Individual cases cause problems as the Organisation's staff member often doesn't see the bigger picture
>
> (Local Authority Head of Housing)

The following statement is interesting as it frames the situation in a way that makes claims of 'efficient and effective' practices which are invisible to an otherwise 'narrow' focus (not seeing the bigger picture) and which therefore were unappreciated by voluntary sector organisations.

> We look at the bigger picture, we have to. When the Organisation defends someone who we are in the process of taking legal action against, then they're undermining our wider strategic function, which is to make sure that rent comes in and that the tenants who do pay rent can have their nice new kitchens and bathrooms, which is what they are entitled to. It's not fair on them and the organisation needs to see it from their perspective ... they need to stand back and look at the bigger picture.
>
> (Local Authority Head of Housing)

There was some sympathy for the Organisation's role in challenging statutory failure, but even when there was acknowledgement of this, the 'bigger picture' trope was used to minimise these shortcomings in favour of more important priorities:

> Working for a local authority means that you can become vary laid back about not being able to meet your duties ... we need organisations ... to put pressure on us when we become too relaxed about all of this. But they also need to see the bigger picture; they also need to be able to see what's important and what's not.
>
> (Local Authority Head of Housing)

The consistency with which respondents referred to the notion of 'not seeing the bigger picture' was remarkable:

> They need to look at the bigger picture, particularly with regard to evictions for rent arrears. The Organisation doesn't appreciate the lengths that landlords go to in order to recover rent. The hoops they jump through for their tenants go largely unnoticed by the Organisation. We are in the business of housing people, not evicting them and we do so only as a last resort. Eviction is seen as a failure for most social landlords.
> (National Housing Membership Organisation)

There was also a hidden, but nonetheless strong, link to notions of performance in the 'bigger picture' discourse. A common thread evident through interviews suggested that housing professionals were doing all they could and that external factors which were imposed upon them through austerity cuts or funding shortages from central government were the principle barrier to running an efficient and effective housing service:

> Working for a local authority means that you can become vary laid back about not being able to meet your duties ... we need organisations ... to put pressure on us when we become too relaxed about all of this. But they also need to see the bigger picture; they also need to be able to see what's important and what's not.
> (Local Authority Head of Housing)

Blame was shifted from institutional failure to one where a distinct lack of resources, units of housing in particular, was the main cause of the inability to adequately discharge duties owed:

> Good legislation is still difficult to implement. [A particular council] has 160,000 people on waiting lists, which makes the 2012 target of ending homelessness5 something of a misnomer. It displaces the problem of homelessness. Rights work fails to acknowledge the good work that is being done by local authorities up and down Scotland. The Organisation needs to see the bigger picture.... They need to acknowledge the difficulties authorities face, both operational and political.
> (Director of Local Authority Landlord Representative Organisation)

There was no doubt that the nature of the professional relationship between statutory housing providers and those organisations that existed to ensure the rights of tenants were met created tension and conflict. It is of interest to note that in this excerpt the source of tension lies in the interpretation by the Chief Housing Officer that 'just causes' are to the 'grubby end' of housing provision what 'idealism' is to 'realism':

> There is an issue whereby the Organisation is seen as having, perhaps, too much of an embattled or combative attitude. Some of the Organisation's staff do not understand the 'grubby end' of housing

> provision and adopt a position of defending 'just causes', which often end in the realisation that there is nothing 'just' about the cause and that what we are dealing with are problems which have much deeper roots. The Organisation's strong brand demonstrates that they deliver high quality services, but they should be quicker to step in and accept there is a problem when the tenant's actions are clearly questionable.
>
> (Local Authority Head of Housing)

There was no capacity here for the commissioning Organisation to respond to these comments and observations, but clear evidence emerged from the interviews with the five participating organisations that highlighted the contradictions created by housing organisations. On the one hand they acknowledged the fact that they were not meeting their statutory obligations and, on the other, that the interventions of the Organisation were counterproductive and damaging to the successful working relations between both institutions.

'Failing to Meet their Statutory Obligations'

All five representatives from the voluntary organisations expressed concerns about the fact that, on a daily basis, local authorities failed to meet their statutory obligations towards those to whom they owed a duty to accommodate under Section II of the *Housing (Scotland) Act 1987* as amended (from here on referred to as 'the Act'). The following example is from a voluntary organisation that worked directly with refugees:

> [Large local authority] is notoriously bad at meeting their statutory obligations. All the local law centres are stretched and it takes about one week just to be seen by an advisor. Therefore [large local authority] is getting away with not meeting their statutory obligations ... this is becoming a great concern to us and a great source of frustration for the caseworkers. So basically, the biggest issue for our clients is a severe lack of good legal advice and advocacy when councils fail to meet their duties and, oh, and a shortage of suitable accommodation. That's the other problem; there are simply not enough units of accommodation to meet demand.
>
> (Housing and Homelessness Organisation)

The following excerpt is from another voluntary organisation:

> Local authorities worry about being taken to task over practice issues, they don't like being challenged for not meeting their duties, and this indirectly improves practice. This can only be a good thing for homeless people.
>
> (Housing and Homelessness Organisation)

It is important to highlight the fact that this interviewee believed that legal challenges, although unpopular with housing professionals, were indeed beneficial to homeless people. The next interviewee highlights the fact that concerns are often ignored:

> Problems in [large local authority] are endemic. People are still being turned away on a daily basis. There is not enough accommodation and [large local authority] pretend to listen to our concerns but at the end of the day they do nothing. The issue is being largely ignored. Things are much worse than they were previously. A statutory service is only as good as its weakest points.
>
> (Housing and Homelessness Organisation)

These concerns were strengthened by another organisation with a similar remit:

> If anything, there's a sense that it's getting worse, you're going to council meetings and you're hearing managers openly discussing the fact that they are failing to meet their statutory obligations, quite openly, without any reservations, and that's really worrying because that would never have happened before. That's a worrying new development.
>
> (Housing and Homelessness Organisation)

The data strongly suggested that two broad concerns were emerging and that these were shared by all the interviewees from the five voluntary organisations who participated:

> The other problem is this distinction which gets made between old homelessness and new homelessness. It's too easy for councils to just bat off criticism. Whenever these new managers are criticised, they say 'oh, that's the old homelessness world', and they bat it off, far too easily. When we raise legitimate concerns about failures in meeting duties, we're criticised as, 'oh you are just looking to cause trouble'.
>
> (Housing and Homelessness Organisation)

It is perhaps significant that the above interviewee believed that certain types and forms of criticism could, in certain circumstances and relating to certain groups, be deflected with relative ease:

> It's far too easy to say, 'oh but look at our list of successes'. [Former head of statutory service] did that for years. Whenever anyone pointed out that they were failing on a daily basis to meet their statutory obligations, [Former head of statutory service] would say, 'yes but look at all our successes'. This is happening all the time

> now; it's just too easy for managers to shrug off criticism. But that 'old homelessness, new homelessness' debate is fascinating to hear, and it's happening in quite high profile places. Previously it was driven by the changes brought in by Housing Options 'are you pro Housing Options or anti Housing Options?', but it has become even more than that and it's 'are you wedded to the legislation or are you open to new ways of working', that's what it seems to be about.
>
> (Housing and Homelessness Organisation)

The concern about legislation is an important one. Local authorities have a statutory obligation to ensure that evictions for rent arrears are an absolute last resort and for those who have been evicted or who find themselves homeless, provide suitable accommodation. What this interviewee seemed to be concerned about was the move away from statutory rights and responsibilities to a more 'flexible' approach that was much less embedded in statute than housing law itself allowed.

Unravelling the Contradictions

The contradictions here, particularly with local authority housing chief housing officers, expose a number of underlying issues in housing services as well as the statutory function which local authorities have in relation to meeting the needs of both those who have accrued rent arrears and of homeless persons. A key issue was the dichotomous position whereby housing professionals (in most cases senior manager or director) made two contradictory points.

The first contradictory point had its own two-fold reality. On one hand, the severe shortage of housing faced by almost every social landlord in the UK provided an unconscious impetus to free-up much needed housing stock by removing those who did not pay they their rent on time. On the other hand, because of this shortage, it generally became extremely difficult, if not impossible, to meet statutory obligations and provide houses when there was a legal obligation to do so.

The second contradiction, which almost always followed on from the first, was that those who found themselves under pressure to either free up accommodation or to refuse applications, then went on to highlight their dismay at having legal challenges made against them for not meeting their own statutory obligations.

In the academic field there has been some exploration of this phenomenon where practitioners and professionals, particularly at a senior level, have held two dichotomous positions. At an academic but nonetheless practical level, Carlen (2008) when writing about her research on criminal justice policies (particularly policies which have 'rehabilitation' as their main objective) highlights the fact that practitioners and professionals simultaneously perform three levels of contradictory action:

- First, they make strong claims that the stated goals of the project are impossible to achieve given the severe resource restrictions;
- Second, they complain about the enormous efforts they have to go to in order to prove the effectiveness of the project; while
- Third, constantly being aware of having to address the 'Other' oppositional reality, that is, what is 'actually happening' at all times, counter to the objectives of the 'official' project (what is supposed to be happening).

This is apparent in the evidence presented above. When housing professionals circumvent the process whereby, they are required to have satisfied the pre-action requirements before seeking decree for eviction, or they refuse to grant someone homelessness status, they mostly do so because of a severe shortage of accommodation and/or resources to deal with the case. In my own role as a Housing Aid Worker, I noticed a strong correlation between falling stock numbers, as Glasgow Housing Association (GHA) demolished some 33,000 units, and a sharp increase in negative homelessness decisions. They both occurred simultaneously. The Chief Housing Officers who participated in this study, talked about being relaxed about not being able to meet their duties acknowledging that they had to prioritise one thing over another (i.e. they could not have both). In short, they were drawing attention to the impossibility of meeting their statutory obligations, given the severe lack of resources available.

The second point is evident in the universal opposition to what participants perceived as being an unnecessarily confrontational and conflictual approach taken by the Organisation. The prevalence of the term 'they don't see the bigger picture' suggested that the housing professionals regarded the Organisation's approach as being unfair, given the circumstances, and the fact that they were, after all, doing their best under what were limiting and restrictive circumstances. There was also a sense that the 'naming and shaming' practices of the Organisation were regarded as unhelpful, since they inflicted reputational damage upon Chief Housing Officers and his or her local authority, thus impeding the 'enormous efforts' they have to go to in order to prove the 'effectiveness of the project'.

Third, the contradictions that arose from the data from these interviews was testament to Carlen's third point. Despite having to make it look 'as if' they were meeting their statutory obligations, the presence of the Organisation and its relentless push to hold them to account complicated the task making life much less straight forward than it otherwise would be. Chief Housing Officers and the institutions that represented their interests were able to tolerate the existence of the Organisation and others like it, but would, it seems from the data, prefer if it was done in such a way that did not challenge either their own practice or that of their institution. This has a distinctly political dimension to it.

Carlen (2008: 9) explains this situation thus:

> Professionals in blame driven cultures ... tend to acquiesce in the pursuit of institutional goals set by the various political and management agendas, at the same time as knowing that they are acquiescing in (and thereby promoting) an imaginary order, the perpetuation of which renders these goals more and more desirable as they become less and less likely of achievement.

It becomes apparent that the perceived 'problem' is, at its core, an issue for the housing professional only. Arguably, the issue of 'naming and shaming' and 'not seeing the bigger picture' has little to do with the commissioning Organisation at all. After all, the Organisation can be said to be doing its job, in the best way it knows how, by holding those in power to account. It does, however, create an unwelcome tension which the Organisation and other third sector organisations with a similar remit, still have to address in some form or other if better working relationships with housing providers are to be built. Particularly those with whom it would hope to engage in future collaborative work.

Housing professionals, like all professionals in all professional fields are able to perform contradictory actions. This is only apparent when viewed from a distance. The objectivist perspective can see the contradictions, but from the subjectivist, insider view, the professionals themselves are too embroiled in the cut and thrust of practice. They are too entangled in the warp and weft of the field, too closely caught up in the 'game' to see that what appears as social relations are actually relations of power. They see only codified practices and collective conventions, rather than ideological devices, and political rhetoric.

Recapitulation

To recap, from the evidence presented in Case Study 1, the housing professionals prioritised the collection of rent and the careful management of arrears, all in the name of the collective good. The external pressures from the legal and regulatory framework that governs evictions, set the priorities that determined the practical realities of how professionals went about managing arrears and evicting people. There was a clear direction of travel. Those interviewees who participated in the research were almost completely unanimous that rent arrears had structural rather than individual causes, yet by the end, no one could 'imagine' an alternative. The last section showed the extent to which the problem of rent arrears was constructed within a justice/fairness binary with the irresponsible tenant (perpetrator) on the one hand and the community of rent paying tenants (victims) on the other. The process of serving notice, going through the motions of meeting the pre-action requirements (when they were adhered to) and taking the case to the Sheriff Court to seek decree for eviction, could be justified when the housing professional could prove, to themselves and others, that all the procedural, technical, and managerial aspects had been carried out.

In this chapter, Case Study 2, the binary was constructed between the housing professionals, trying their best under difficult circumstances, and the overzealous, righteous and shortsighted housing rights workers, who were not only making things worse but were incapable of understanding the rules of the game. The corrosiveness of naming and shaming, coupled with the shortsightedness of not seeing the bigger picture, were framed in a way that allowed the housing professional, particularly those who occupied favourable positions as Chief Housing Officers or Directors of Housing Associations, to shift the blame onto the Organisation, for their own failures in meeting their statutory obligations.

The inclusion of excerpts from the interview data provided by other rights-based housing and homelessness organisations provided a degree of balance in that it became evident that there was widespread concern that local authorities and their representative bodies were falling short of the mark when it came to meeting their statutory obligations.

What emerged from this case study was the difficulties presented by the idea that the statutory sector – responsible for the provision of housing services as well as overseeing evictions – could form workable and functioning partnerships with voluntary organisations charged with enforcing the discharge of these very same statutory provisions. What the evidence from this case study shows, is that notions of collaboration, partnership, and/or joined-up working were at best misplaced and, probably more realistically, founded upon the 'common sense' naivety, embedded within liberal tropes and ideologies.

Although both sectors appear to locate tenants and homeless people as the central concern of their professional practice, they have different priorities concerning these two groups. It is this slight gap that becomes amplified through the passing of time. And the assertion of each group's own distinctive priorities leads to the levels of friction, misunderstanding and ultimately animosity and conflict that defines relations between what would otherwise appear to the casual observer as very similar organisations, doing very similar jobs, on behalf of the same group of people.

References

Carlen P. (Ed.) (2008) *Imaginary Penalties*, London: Willan Publishers.

Crawford J. (2015) 'The (unintended) consequences of governance? Examining the role of 'Frames' in creating Imaginary housing systems and their importance for understanding the practices of senior housing professionals', *Housing Theory and Society*, 32 (3): 302–319.

Holt K. and Kelly N. (2018) 'Limits to partnership working: Developing relationship-based approaches with children and their families', *Journal of Social Welfare and Family Law*, 40 (2): 147–163.

Manzi T. and Smith-Bowers B. (2004) So many managers, so little vision: Registered social landlords and consortium schemes in the UK. *European Journal of Housing Policy*, 4 (1): 57–75.

Raco M. (2016) *State-led Privatisation and the Demise of the Democratic State: Welfare Reform and Localism in an Era of Regulatory Capitalism*, London: Routledge.
Schmachtel S. (2015) 'Local partnerships as "rationalized myths": A critical examination of the micro-discourse in educational partnership working', *Critical Policy Studies*, 10 (4): 448–467.
Wacquant L. (2009) *Punishing the Poor: The Neoliberal Government of Social Insecurity*, Durham: Duke University Press.

6 'They Want Us to Become Immigration Officers. It's Not Our Role'

Case Study 3: Creating a Hostile Environment for Immigrants

In order to appreciate the nuanced nature of the evidence presented in this, the third case-study, it is necessary to set the political and legislative context within the wider issue of immigration. This includes the UKs pervasive policy of creating a 'hostile environment' for '*illegal* immigrants', which as will become evident, extends to becoming a hostile environment for 'all' immigrants.

The political context from which this case-study emerged is characterised by a rise in 'right wing populism' in the mainstream political sphere in the UK, as well as the US and other parts of Europe. From Trump's pledge to 'build a wall' to keep out the Mexicans, and the right-wing of the UK Conservative Party's successful bid to 'take back control of our borders' by leaving the European Union, as well as the creation of a 'hostile environment for immigrants', it is clear that anti-immigration rhetoric now resonates loudly on both sides of the Atlantic.

The Windrush 'scandal' in the UK sums up perfectly this rightward tilting of the state in recent years. When the Empire Windrush arrived from the Caribbean in 1948, the new arrivals were welcomed into a model of economic organisation that required a substantial influx of immigrant labour. As the political economy transitioned from its industrial base to one founded upon the supremacy of finance and rentier capitalism, immigrants became a 'surplus group' increasingly 'constructed' as a threat not only to jobs and housing, but to the British way of life. Of the cases that are known, around 83 people were wrongly detained and deported as part of what has been termed the 'Windrush Scandal', leading to renewed debate on the ethics of the existence of the UKs deportation targets and the heavy-handed practices of the Home Office.

These cases not only highlight the extent of public outrage at the forced removal of immigrants, torn from the communities in which they had made their homes, it also proves that the right-wing populism that put the wind in the sales of the UK government was not a universal political force. There was, however, an evident shift towards a new punitiveness in government policy and practice. Although the anti-immigration rhetoric has been ratcheted-up in the last decade, it has its origins in a much longer trajectory in which the rightward tilting of the bureaucratic state was augmented during the period of New Labour's rule. Indeed, as early as 2008 Labour's Immigration Minister Liam Byrne said: "What we are proposing here will, I think, flush illegal migrants out. We are trying to create a much more hostile environment in this country if you are here illegally" (Hansard, 2018).

The 'hostile environment policy' introduced by the Conservative government implemented and oversaw an administrative and legislative programme designed to directly target the immigrant population in order to root out and remove those who were resident in the UK without legal 'right to remain'. The punitive measures that accompanied the UK *Immigration Acts of 2014* and *2016* were first voiced by Theresa May in 2012 when she said: "the aim is to create, here in Britain, a really hostile environment for illegal immigrants" (Crawford, McKee and Leahy, 2019).

From the perspective of the UK Conservative government, illegal immigration is an 'ongoing problem', which it seeks to further address through the *Immigration Act 2016*. For opposition parties, the devolved governments of Scotland, Wales and Northern Ireland, as a well as church groups, charities and other stakeholder agencies, the problem of 'illegal immigration' is grossly exaggerated (Crawford, Leahy and McKee, 2019). What is jointly acknowledged, however, is that there is at present a humanitarian crisis involving the mass migration of refugees and asylum seekers fleeing to Europe (see for example, Abbasi et al., 2015; Albahari, 2015).

The Home Office (2016) justifies the necessity of introducing the 2016 Act by stating that the previous *Immigration Act 2014*, although fairly comprehensive, does not go far enough in reducing 'illegal immigration' in the UK. The new 'powers', which the 2016 Act proposes are, the Home Office claims, designed to actively deny 'illegal immigrants' access to employment markets and a variety of 'services' within the UK, including housing and banking facilities. Indeed, the Act goes beyond simply targeting 'illegal' immigrants, as Part 7 ensures that all customer facing, public sector workers will speak fluent English. The 2016 Act prescribes that a 'special helpline' be set up so that members of the public can report public sector workers whose English language skills do not meet the required standard.

Section 1 of the Act is concerned with the labour market and illegal labour abuse and enforcement: making it a criminal offence to work without documentation, seizing illegal workers' earnings as the proceeds of crime, making it easier to prosecute employers, and making sanctions tougher. Part 2 deals with 'access to services' including residential tenancies, driving licences and bank accounts. According to the Government, Part 2 of the Act, building on the right to rent provisions first outlined for England in the *2014 Immigration Act*, makes it more difficult to live and work in the UK without documentation. It does so by making it easier for private landlords to evict migrant tenants who are not legally in the country, and by creating a new criminal offence for dishonest landlords and agents who exploit migrants and repeatedly fail to carry out right-to-rent checks. The Act also ensures that those unlawfully present in the UK are unable to drive. It also requires banks and building societies to take action against existing account holders who are unlawfully residing in the UK, thus placing an obligation on banks and building societies to carry out periodic checks of the immigration status of existing current account holders. One of the other areas of significant change is contained within Part 4, which makes it easier to remove those who have no right to remain within the UK. The Act proposes to force those who wish to lodge an appeal against a deportation decision, to do so from the country from which they entered the UK. This will result in those wishing to appeal being removed from the UK before any appeal process is permitted to begin.

These proposed new regulations present a multitude of state strategies to make the life of migrants, both those who are 'legal' and 'illegal' in the eyes of the State, more contentious and precarious, bestowing a slew of regulatory mechanisms that migrants must overcome to acquire a place to stay, access banking services, acquire the ability to drive, and secure public employment. Furthermore, it shifts the responsibility of scrutiny and adherence onto landlords, bank employees and public sector managers in efforts to discharge policing and accountability to lay citizens. This liability is further entrenched by threats of extensive fines and custodial sentences for landlords who fail to monitor and comply with the Act's punitive agenda.

Background to the Research

The research that forms the basis of this case-study was designed as a seedcorn project, with the intention that the data produced would inform a much larger funding application focused on in-depth research on the impact of the *Immigration Act*. It forms part of an ongoing project. The initial phase of this research sought out key actors in both the social and private housing sectors of Scotland and England. The 2016 Act was implemented in England, and at the time of the study had yet to be enacted by the Secretary of State for Scotland (for whom the 2014 Act was the most recent).

Our research began with a review of the briefing papers and written responses to the Government's consultation on the *Immigration Act 2016*. We found a number of key themes, which linked almost all of the responses. These revolved around the perceived change to the role of the landlord, the effect on devolved legal competency in Scotland, financial implications for landlords, particularly around the issue of evictions, and discrimination. This latter issue was of most relevance to this study as it addressed concerns that the Right to Rent prescriptions of the *Immigration Acts of 2014* and *2016* would further disadvantage groups who already faced disproportionate levels of discrimination in the housing sector. Additionally, having a discriminating effect on marginalised groups who, although not immigrants, were unable to obtain the evidence required to prove that they had leave to remain in the UK.

The research was carried out in two phases with in-depth semi-structured interviews being carried out with 22 key actors with experience of cases involving the Right to Rent part of Immigration Acts in both Scotland and England. The sample spread is shown here in Table 6.1.

The hour-long interviews explored the main concerns that emerged from the briefing papers and consultation responses, as well as probing other areas of relevance. Participants' accounts were anonymised and individuals are referred to in the discussion that follows by their job title and organisation. The interview data collected were imported into the qualitative analysis software NVivo 10 and scrutinised for emerging themes. Those related specifically to the changing role of the landlord and the issue of discrimination form the focus of this case-study.

Presenting the Evidence

The *Immigration Acts* had both direct and indirect effects on housing and evictions in the UK. Directly, the process of responsibilisation through criminalisation served to impose upon landlords' new duties, which almost all of them opposed. Indirectly, the Acts represented a mechanism of exclusion and discrimination, something the interviewees seemed less than happy about, with many claiming it was entirely antithetical to the spirit of housing provision and the legislative framework that underpinned the housing system in the UK. These two effects are inextricably linked. As well as opposing the imposition of duties they previously had no obligation to carry out, landlords and organisations working with immigrant groups also opposed the fact that the Right to Rent part of the Act forced landlords to either refuse to accommodate those whose immigration status they were unsure of, as well as being forced to evict tenants who could not, for whatever reason, prove they had leave to remain in the UK.

Table 6.1 Participants in the Right to Rent Project

Generic job role	*Participants*
Local authority housing organisation	4
Immigration law/migrant advice	4
Private landlord organisation	4
PRS housing advice	3
Policy and practice organisations/ Experts with focus on migration	2
Charity organisation	2
Housing activists	2
Local authority enforcement	1
Total	22

Having systematically analysed a wide range of briefing papers and consultation responses from key stakeholders in Scotland and England, the main theme unifying all participants was one of direct opposition to the Right to Rent prescriptions of the *Immigration Acts of 2014* and *2016*. There were many reasons for this opposition that were reiterated in the qualitative interviews (for a more detailed discussion see Crawford, Leahy and McKee, 2016, 2019; Leahy, McKee and Crawford, 2018). Of concern among participants was the strongly held belief that immigration control was simply not the landlord's responsibility. In England, 82% of members of the Residential Landlords Association (RLA), a body representing the interests of private sector landlords, opposed the Immigration Act. A House of Commons Briefing Paper on the issue, openly admitted it was 'controversial among landlords', and reported the fact that most social landlords who took part in the consultation opposed the plan (Bate and Ota, 2016). One consistent claim made in all the interviews, as well as most of the written submissions and briefing papers, was that the extension of immigration duties to landlords and social housing organisations was inappropriate since it was not within the remit of housing to conduct immigration checks, as this quote exemplifies:

> No, definitely not. It is not a landlord's role. Maybe it conflicts with devolution, but I don't think the aims of the Housing Acts in Scotland are all that different to the aims of housing legislation south of the border.
>
> (Housing Association 4)

This comment highlights an important convention, collectively held by those interviewed, that what immigration officers do and what housing officers do are entirely different, if not completely antithetical. The interviewee above acknowledged a shared ethos between social housing providers beyond the confines of Scotland, to include the UK and Europe. This creates something of a 'generalized' or 'meta' opposition between the field of housing on one hand and the field of immigration control on the other. It is important to note that the *connection* between the demands of the *Immigration Acts* and the requirement of housing professionals to become immigration officials or border guards was made universally, both in the Scottish and in the English samples. Not only was the opposition to the Right to Rent part of the Act shared by both Scottish and English landlords, there was no difference in attitude between private and social landlords, as this next example from an English PRS landlord representative shows.

> I don't think it's appropriate for a landlord to be the person to turn around and say, no, your papers aren't in order ... to have to be the person to knock on the door of what is their home and say you're no longer allowed

> to live here, which is the state at the moment with right to rent. I think it puts landlords and tenants in a very, very awkward position.
>
> (Private Landlord Organisation 2)

Reinforcing this point, this next interviewee situated the prescriptions of the Right to Rent legislation in direct opposition to what they saw as their function in the social housing field. The binary here is juxtaposed between supporting people to sustain their tenancy by helping them settle into the community on one hand, and the requirement for them to do exactly the opposite if tenants cannot provide evidence that they have leave to remain on the other:

> Yes, we become immigration officials and that is not why people work in housing. Absolutely not. It is not our role. We are here to help people. How can we start a tenancy off saying 'we are here to support you? Let's do everything we can to help you. Let's help you access other services. Let's sort out your benefits. Let's get you engaged in the local community. Welcome!' And then a year later we're saying, well, sorry we want you out. That is not our role.
>
> (Housing Association 1)

This Housing Association manager juxtaposed the role of the housing professional, itself conceptualised as 'being there to help people', with the role of the immigration official that was referred to indirectly with reference to enforcing evictions. These two 'actions' are part of the same binary which, linked by the issue of housing (either providing housing or depriving people of their housing), places the roles of housing officer and immigration officer in direct opposition to each other. This opposition makes it difficult for housing professionals to justify what they perceive to be an unnecessary and arbitrary decision to deny housing to a household on the grounds of immigration status.

Expressing the tension between the provision of accommodation and management of housing (a civic good), and the need to carry out immigration checks, the next interview extract emphasizes the unfairness of the *Immigration Act* from a landlord's perspective.

> I think landlords are put in a very invidious position, because they are not just the providers of accommodation, but become a bit of a proxy immigration officer and they are not trained to do that, they didn't ask to do that, and I think it is very unfair for the government to expect that.
>
> (Third Sector Organisation 1)

Framing the situation as an injustice, the above interviewee outlined the problem of turning housing officers into immigration officers by extending the state's border control functions to include institutions with no previous involvement in such practices. This reconfiguration of the role of housing professionals, and indeed the sector more broadly, was strongly resisted by our interviewees, as the quote below illuminates:

> They want us to become immigration officers. It's not our role. Certainly not and that is not why we are here, we do not do that at the moment, and that is not what we are going to do.
>
> (Housing Association 2)

Understanding resistance is crucial to understanding how 'actually existing neoliberalism' plays itself out on the ground. Yet there has been little focus on the resistance among frontline workers in the housing field (for exceptions see Casey and Allen 2004, and McKee 2009). The view that rejected the imposition of immigration control duties upon landlords also existed beyond the immediate field of the landlords themselves, as this next example shows:

> I don't think it's right to turn private landlords, and housing associations into border control agents.
>
> (Immigration Law/Migrant Advice 2)

The next example highlights the contractual nature of the tenancy agreement, which (to the mind of the housing professional) was built upon reciprocal relations of trust. The following comment from a housing manager invoked the centrality of the contract between landlord and tenant. The tenancy agreement was the justificatory focus here, encapsulating the 'rights-based' approach upon which traditional forms of social housing were founded. For the housing manager below, the ethos of rights and responsibilities was central to a sense of social justice and fairness for all, undergirding the civic order of worth encapsulated in the contract.

> There is nothing in our tenancy agreement about immigration. So, all we are asking people is that they observe the conditions of their tenancy and if they do then they won't run the risk of us trying to repossess the property. The tenancy agreement is a fundamental contract involving the rights and the responsibilities of the landlord and tenant. You keep to your half of the bargain and we will keep to ours, that's the deal.
>
> (Housing Association 1)

Tying the triadic nexus of landlord, tenant and community together, this interviewee draws on a number of principles such as community development and social cohesion. The singling out of individuals for extraordinary or special treatment is a practice that is entirely antithetical to the principles that facilitate community. This trait of 'hierarchizing' worthy individuals above those who are less worthy, divides people into deserving and undeserving groups, in order to 'police' them, and make 'special rules' for some tenants while leaving others alone.

> Yes. There is a regulatory element to this Right to Rent thing, almost a police officer role. [The government and the regulator] have been after a community development, social cohesion approach ... so to divide people and say, well you can come in and you can't, and you have got special rules and you haven't, and when we knock on the door it might be to say you can't stay here anymore. It changes the relationship between you and the tenants and the community.
>
> (Third Sector Organisation 1)

The language represented in this next interview extract, centred on the desire to make communities stable by fostering ways in which tenants could settle into safe accommodation which could provide a long-term solution.

> No. I don't think it is a landlord's role. I think a landlord's role is to provide safe accommodation that people can view as a long-term home. We want people to settle in this community. We want the community to be stable. I definitely do not think it's our role to be implementing the work of the Home Office.
>
> (Housing Association 2)

Since evicting tenants was regarded as a last resort, housing professionals were concerned that criminalising the landlord would induce them to make unjust, unethical and perhaps unlawful attempts to engage in the process of 'summary eviction'. This justification, below, was challenged when an eviction takes place, not for reasons of 'behaviour', but simply because of a person's immigration status.

> This doesn't make sense, but yet we are going to be compelled to do it, and it will make some members of staff incredibly uncomfortable and perhaps not want to engage with it. If it becomes a process and a procedure around taking someone to court, most people will say 'that's not why I came to work in housing. I don't want to be a part of this'. What do you do then? It becomes quite difficult maintaining staff morale and that kind of thing.
>
> (Housing Association 3)

Moving from personal preference to collective convention by invoking a sense of civic responsibility did not, for the stakeholders at least, simply apply to the work done by social landlords, it extended to other areas such as the private rented housing sector. Recent legislation in Scotland now affords private sector tenants greater security of tenure – a right that is undermined by the Right to Rent (for further discussion, see Crawford,

Leahy and McKee, 2016). *The Private Housing (Tenancies) (Scotland) Act 2016* removed the ability of landlords to end a tenancy without having grounds (laid down in this legislation) to do so. Its' implementation in 2017 augmented tenants' security of tenure by replacing the Short Assured Tenancy (SAT) with the Scottish Private Residential Tenancy (SPRT).

> If they go ahead with what is proposed in England, where a landlord can summarily evict, that completely undermines the messages from the Private Housing (Tenancies) (Scotland) Act 2016. The whole point about that was to get a very clear message to private landlords that every eviction has to be subject to due legal process.... If we are then saying 'except for this one where you can just evict people by knocking on the door'. I think [the Immigration Act] reinforces all of that bad practice about illegal evictions which we have been trying to eliminate.
>
> (Third Sector Organisation 1)

The objections to the 'discriminatory' language used in the *Immigration Act 2016* all had civic undertones, as it was seen to encourage practices that involved the demonization of certain groups, singling people out as 'exceptional' in so far as they were deemed 'illegal'. This sits in direct opposition to the language of community cohesion and social inclusion that underpins a sense of civic value. Although no one articulated the issue as such, there seemed to be something of a problem with current immigration control rhetoric, shifting the criminalising gaze from 'behaviour' to 'status' (for a fuller debate on this aspect of immigration control, see Malloch and Rigby, 2016).

> We wouldn't use the term 'illegal' migrants or 'failed' asylum seekers because that in itself implies that the person is illegal or that the person has, in some way, failed. We prefer to use the term 'people with irregular immigration status'.... For many years we have been campaigning against the term 'illegal immigrant' or 'illegal migrant'. Our position is that people can't be illegal. It's possible to have done something illegal, but it is not possible to 'be illegal'. This legislation is smattered with the terms, which when we read it, we find quite offensive.
>
> (Third Sector Organisation 2)

This interviewee makes a profound observation. The Council of Europe has advised that the UK should stop using terminology such as 'illegal' migrants and 'failed asylum seekers', and instead use much more neutral language such as 'undocumented migrants' or 'people with irregular immigration status' (Malloch, 2016). This level of discrimination goes beyond mere language, translating into discriminatory practice across the housing sector. As well as opposition to being coerced through criminalisation, in becoming border guards, and the possibility of having to evict tenants on account of their 'status', the participants were unanimous in their criticism of the fact that the Acts created even more levels of discrimination, in a sector where discrimination was already a problem.

> You've got effectively a large unskilled body of people who aren't used to looking at immigration documents who are then supposed to be able to distinguish between different kinds of documents of which there are dozens. So, I think it was a mistake from the beginning to impose that responsibility on private landlords ... the fact that the penalties are severe is bound to deter people from exercising any flexibility.
>
> (Policy and Practice Organisation 1)

Private sector participants were very aware of the fact that the criminalising aspect of the Act would deter landlords from letting to those whose status they were not certain of.

> The whole purpose of the Immigration Act is the biggest piece of discriminatory legislation I think I have ever seen.... You are not going to rent to people if you think that the very act of renting to them is going to land you with either a civil penalty or a criminal offence if you get it wrong.
>
> (Private Rented Sector Advice Agency 1)

It was also widely acknowledged that rather than affect those who were here without leave to remain, the punitive and coercive dimensions of the Immigration Acts would discriminate against all immigrants, as well as minorities who held British passports:

> This legislation has sent another signal that in fact legislation will discriminate against people of colour and ethnic minorities in general, even though it's supposedly aimed at what the Government calls people here illegally.
>
> (Housing Activist 1)

There was acknowledgement that in a market that had more renters than landlords, then landlords simply would not take risks, further disadvantaging minority groups:

> You can certainly imagine circumstances where you've got a high demand area.... If you've got ten applicants, eight of whom have a passport, you immediately recognise as something that means you are definitely not committing a criminal offence and two, that it would take you an hour to go away and check, I can imagine the property goes to people who are easy to process.
>
> (Private Rented Sector Organisation 2)

The issue participants had with this level of discrimination was that in addition to creating vulnerability through discrimination, it had an exacerbatory effect on those who were already vulnerable or had the potential to become so:

> Those who perhaps have children or who have health needs or have additional vulnerabilities in addition to their insecure immigration status, I think ultimately, yes, it could have an impact, more negative impact on them. I think maybe they would be at higher risk of looking towards more unsuitable living arrangements.
>
> (Immigration Law/Migrant Advice 1)

Ultimately, as well as being opposed to the imposition of border guard duties, the pressure to evict people, and all the issues of direct and indirect discrimination, there was an almost universal acknowledgement of the complete futility of it all. Ultimately, few if any of the respondents could see how the punitive and criminalising legislation would do anything other than make an already problematic system even worse while benefiting groups who operated underground, and who were already involved in unlawful practices.

> Instead of it tackling any perceived immigration problems, what it is actually doing is allowing that landlord to buy his third Mercedes. It's feeding a massive criminal market who don't care about the council, they don't care about enforcement, because you can never point the finger at exactly who they are anyway.
>
> (Private Rented Sector Advice 1)

Experts in related professions talked about the futility of enforcing legislation that did nothing to address the actual issue, while putting more and more people at risk.

> Potentially the lack of housing being available to them doesn't trigger them to leave, it ultimately puts them in more risky situations.
>
> (Immigration Law/Migrant Advice 2)

There was also acknowledgment that, for the majority of undocumented migrants, failed asylum seekers and others fleeing persecution, the situation they would be returning to was so dangerous, they would be driven underground in the UK in order to avoid the perils that any return home might entail:

> I think that the provision of accommodation comes quite a long way down people's list of what makes them think about staying.
>
> (Policy and Practice Organisation 3)

Recapitulation

The Right to Rent provisions of the *Immigration Acts of 2014* and *2016* are an integral part of the UK's 'hostile environment' policy for dealing with immigration. Despite its claims to focus attention on 'illegal' immigrants, the draconian punishments for non-compliance are so severe that the Acts place a significant risk on landlords who may be unsure of the tenant's immigration status. This, the data suggests, leads to increased levels of discrimination in a market that already suffers from unequal outcomes for some groups who find themselves with diminishing options as housing becomes scarcer and more expensive as gentrification expands through the cities of the UK.

The landlords and related professionals who participated in this research were unanimous in their condemnation of the Right to Rent. First, they opposed the imposition of immigration control duties, claiming that they were not border guards, but rather that they were landlords and housing professionals. In short, they saw the spirit that underpinned their role being one in which they were providers of housing, not deprivers of housing. Second, most of the participants were uncomfortable with the discriminatory aspect of the legislation, with many questioning the morality of treating certain groups differently. As was evident in the first case study, evictions could be justified when the tenant's actions could be held to account, but this justification became much more difficult when they were being forced to evict someone because of their status. Third, many viewed the Right to Rent as just another politically motivated state intervention that was not only ineffective, but would make matters worse, create precarity when none previously existed, and force the issue underground. Ultimately, those who would benefit most would be those landlords who operate unlawfully, in the unregulated end of the market.

The interviews yielded a number of insights. These exist on two levels. Firstly, there are insights that arose from the phenomenological relation between the landlord on one hand and the rules and legislative interventions that emanated from the state on the other. These insights came from the lived experiences of landlords, housing and other related professionals and, took the form of opinions and points of view, representing the subjective understanding people had of the very particular social universe that they found themselves immersed in. This relation, between the landlord and the regulatory state, appeared in the data in the form of a resistance/enforcement binary. This partially explains why Theresa May augmented the already draconian 2014 Act in 2016, by increasing the punishment to five years in prison for those who refused to comply with the enforcement of a 'hostile environment' for immigrants.

One of the effects of the *Immigration Acts* was to codify people into specific social categories and extend surveillance throughout society, enlisting citizens in border protection practices. In accordance with this, individuals are now seen to embody the border, carrying it with them, as individuals embodying encoded boundaries. Discursive and material bordering processes heighten suspicion, which means that individuals are viewed as bodies to mistrust, bodies that are in need of surveillance, control, and extraction from the State. The Right to Rent system actualises these sentiments through the tenant immigration checking system. It is this embodiment of the border that the *Immigration Act* both produces and relies on to perform its governing function. This distinction draws on landlords' notions of who is part of the territory and who is not, leading them to make determinations by initially relying on who embodies the border for them.

The historical processes that have shaped these codifications, have been accompanied by the rightward tilting of the state, a phenomenon that will be explored in the next section. This rightward tilting has been accompanied by a rise, not only in the UK but all over Europe and indeed the US, of far-right political factions and tropes. These have combined to create, here in the UK, not only the subjectivities that can facilitate a 'hostile environment' for immigrants, but the desire to leave the European Union on account of the fact that membership compromises the UK's sovereignty with regard to its borders. By augmenting anti-immigration sentiment, both the Conservative and indeed Blair and Brown's Labour Party, and the disproportionate amount of media coverage given to Nigel Farage and his UK Independence Party, created the perfect conditions to tilt the balance of opinion in favour of leaving the EU (see also Virdee and McGeever, 2017).

Of the rhetorical devices employed by the Vote Leave campaign in the EU referendum in 2016, 'taking back control of our borders', was perhaps one that resonated the most. However, it must be noted that although England and Wales voted overwhelmingly to leave the EU, Scotland and Northern Ireland voted by a decent margin to remain. Indeed, it can be said that the Scottish population has an entirely different view of immigrants and immigration than that of much of England. On 27 January 2020, the First Minister of Scotland made a formal request that Scotland be given powers over immigration (a power reserved to Westminster) with the introduction of a Scottish visa allowing immigrants free movement into Scotland after Brexit. This was immediately refused by the Westminster Government.

The rightward tilting of the state is not something that is simply accepted without question or challenge. Indeed, as we have seen from the evidence in this case-study, active resistance is and always has been a reality among housing and related professionals. The data presented here as evidence also shows the extent to which changing attitudes is a far more effective way to bring about changes in behaviour than policing and punishment. The evidence presented here shows that the state can coerce professional groups into adopting 'policing and punishing' roles, by enacting laws designed to police and punish the professional groups themselves. When cruel state policies designed to punish certain groups (immigrants) are enforced by cruel state policies designed to punish certain groups (those who may assist immigrants), questions inevitably arise as to the kind of society we (want to) live in.

What is perhaps striking is the fact that despite the criminalisation of landlords who failed to comply with the *Immigration Act of 2014* and *2016* and despite the severe penalties, the objections presented by landlords centred on the fact that 'border policing' and the discriminatory practices this entailed, was simply not in their remit. This, remit, their role, the reason they did what they did, the meanings they derived from their work as housing professionals and as landlords, held more significance than the threat of imprisonment. 'Meaning', and not indeed a fear of losing one's liberty, seemed to be the central driving force behind professionals and landlord's actions. The reason for this will be explored in Part III.

References

Abbasi K., Patel K. and Godlee F. (2015) 'Europe's refugee crisis: An urgent call for moral leadership'. *BMJ*, 351: h4833.

Albahari M. (2015) 'Europe's refugee crisis. *Anthropology Today*, 31: 1–2.

Bate A. and Ota S. (2016) *Right to Rent: Private landlords' Duty to Carry Out Immigration Status Checks*, Briefing Paper No. SN07025, 12 February. London: House of Commons Library.

Casey R. and Allen C. (2004) 'Social housing managers and the performance ethos: Towards a "professional project of the self"'. *Work, Employment and Society*, *18* (2): 395–412.

Crawford J., Leahy S. & McKee K. (2016) 'The Immigration Act and the 'Right to Rent': Exploring governing tensions within and beyond the state'. *People, Place and Policy Online*, *10* (2): 114–125.

Crawford J., McKee K. & Leahy S. (2019) 'The Right to Rent: Active resistance to evolving geographies of state regulation'. *International Journal of Urban and Regional Research*, https://doi.org/10.1111/1468-2427.12731.

Crawford J., Leahy S. & McKee K. (2019) 'More than a hostile environment: Exploring the impact of the Right to Rent part of the Immigration Act 2016'. *Sociological Research Online*, https://doi.org/10.1177/1360780419867708.

Hansard (2018) UK Parliament 25 April 2018, *Prime Minister: Oral Questions to Answers*, Volume 638.

Home Office (2016) *Immigration Act 2016*. www.gov.uk/government/collections/immigration-bill-2015-16.

Leahy S., McKee K. & Crawford J. (2018) 'Generating confusion, concern, and precarity through the Right to Rent Scheme in Scotland'. *Antipode*, *50* (3): 604–620.

Malloch M. (2016) 'Criminalising victims of human trafficking: State responses and punitive practices', in M. Malloch and P. Rigby (Eds), *Human Trafficking: The Complexities of Exploitation*, Edinburgh University Press, Edinburgh.

Malloch M. and Rigby P. (Eds) (2016) *Human Trafficking: The Complexities of Exploitation*, Edinburgh University Press, Edinburgh.

McKee K. (2009) 'Regulating Scotland's social landlords: Localized resistance to technologies of performance management'. *Housing Studies*, *24* (2): 155–171.

Virdee S. and McGeever B. (2017) 'Racism, crisis, Brexit'. *Ethnic and Racial Studies*, 41: 1802–1819.

Part III

The Practice of Housing

7 Constructing a Theoretical Model

Exposition

This third and final section of the book will move on from the People of Housing, to focus on the issue of Housing Practice. The first section, the World of Housing provided the context for evictions by describing the legal and regulatory framework that governs all aspects of housing, as well as the wider political economy from which it arose. The last section, in the form of three case-studies, presented the evidence from those working in the housing sector who were, in some capacity, involved in evictions. By taking seriously the views and opinions of housing and related professionals it was possible to form a picture of common forms of practice and gain access to collective conventions that underpinned professional practice in each particular case.

Given that each research participant was interviewed individually, the frequency with which very specific tropes, expressed through shared values and justifications arose, was itself worthy of note. Indeed, the thematic content of the interviews had a regularity and consistency that suggests something more than merely the individual 'subjective' views of housing professionals, expressed in an interview. What appears to have emerged from the data is evidence that within specific groups of professionals, there exists sets of codified practices that not only shape what they do, but also shape the way they think about and understand what they do.

Individual housing professionals have strong personal views, opinions and feelings about their roles as housing professionals. However, it is clear that in order to justify their actions, particularly in regard to an emotive and challenging issue such as evictions, they communicate these justifications through a collectively recognised and codified set of frames. What this chapter will do is to devise a theory/method nexus that not only facilitates engagement with these frames, but also enables a degree of analysis. In-depth examination will take place in Chapter 8, but for now, the focus of attention will be on the construction of a theoretical framework for identifying, engaging and analysing the evidence presented by the housing professionals who took part in these research projects.

Development

This chapter will exploit the rich vein of social thought that has been mined and developed in both Europe and the US over the last century or so. From the pioneering work of Marx, Weber and Durkheim, a critical paradigm emerged that was developed by symbolic interactionists such as Mead, Blumer and Goffman, before being refined further by the Frankfurt School refugees as well as a range of philosophers and social scientists including Elias, Foucault, and Bourdieu. The ensuing synthesis will enmesh the combined efforts of these 'critical theorists' with the more modern forms of social psychology such as those developed by proponents of the popular movement currently exploring Moral Foundations Theory and its relevance to understanding modern society. Before adding contemporary social psychological developments to the mix, it is necessary to capture the key principles of the more traditional 'critical paradigm'. The critical tradition that emerged from the 20th century is invaluable in that it not only accounts for the hidden forms of power that operate under the radar of common-sense perception, but it places a strong emphasis on the operation of symbolic power in all its various forms.

It is this 'critical' contribution that places serious doubt on the use value of common sense or liberal perspectives within social science, since they are limited to the apprehension of the superficial 'appearance of things', merely accounting for the illusory nature of reality. Adapting a Hegelian concept, Marx famously pointed out in Volume III of *Capital* (2003 [1894]: 797) that "all science would be superfluous if the outward appearance and the essence of things directly coincided". Bluntly put, nothing in the world is ever as it seems, a point that merely serves to emphasise why a 'critical' approach is required in order to compensate for the inherent weakness of the mainstream, liberal perspective that currently dominates the field of housing studies. This division or dichotomy is between what the Frankfurt School philosophers and social scientists called 'critical' reason and 'instrumental' reason, with the former being better suited to scientific enquiry than the latter, which is associated with common sense.

An approach is therefore required, that can not only apprehend the dimensions of power that persist in their obscure and obfuscated form, but to place a radical doubt upon all that exists in the world in an 'unquestioned' state. This radical doubt, is an essential thinking tool, since one of the main functions of 'power' in both its material and symbolic forms, is to make the completely 'arbitrary' and 'historically contingent' nature of reality appear as 'natural' and 'necessary'. The State employs a wide range of technologies for making that which is arbitrary (it could always have been otherwise) such as the 'law', 'constitutional tradition', 'educational curricula', 'forms of measurement', 'borders' etc., seem perfectly natural, when of course there is absolutely nothing natural about any of them. They are all political constructions. This process of naturalisation through obfuscation gives that which is 'historically contingent' a sense of necessity by ascribing the outcomes and results of fights between individuals, struggles between groups, and wars between countries with a deep sense of inevitability. That it had to happen. In short, powerful groups are able to 'universalise' their 'particular' worldview, through a process of legitimisation.

Transversely, this chapter will construct a critical ontology by drawing on a number of interrelated principles in order to weave together a theoretical framework that can not only account, but can compensate for, the weakness of the liberal approach. First, as the Materialists and the Symbolic Interactionists after them pointed out, there is no true nature of reality 'out there', waiting to be discovered, it is constructed by human beings in their social interactions. Second, although it is true that people construct their own reality, they do not do so 'freely', under the conditions of their choosing, a fact that places structural limitations on all forms of human action including thought. Third, society, although perceived as a macrostructure, consists of a vast assemblage of microstructures ('worlds' or 'fields') that combine to facilitate action and interaction through the generation of symbolically meaningful networks, language forms and collective conventions, from which knowledge and human practices arise.

In short, the theoretical model proposed is founded upon the principles of symbolic interactionism. This is a model in which humans relate to things based on the meanings they have for them, that these meanings arise out of human interactions and that an interpretive process is employed when people deal with their external environment. The ontology of the symbolic interactionists that this form of structural constructivism invokes, recognises that the world is made up of three types of object; *physical objects* (nature, man-made structures, bounded territories), *social objects* (managers, mothers, students) and *abstract objects* (ideas, concepts and moral principles). Indeed, as Karl Popper (1978) points out, these three types of object correspond to three distinct worlds. World One is the physical reality within which humans exist. World Two is the subjective, or phenomenological experience of that physical reality, which exists in mental states and perceptions. World Three is the body of human knowledge and practice that exists intersubjectively, collectively held, but beyond the grasp of any single subjective experience of it. Thus, knowledge and human practice arise from the interaction between people and the worlds they inhabit in a process that is thoroughly dialectical (Berger and Luckman, 1991 [1966]). It can be said to be dialectical insofar as each world changes in correspondence to changes in the other worlds. As Hegel insightfully reflects, "it is a characteristic of societies to produce their own environment and to be transformed by the transformations of the environment they transform" (quoted in Bourdieu, 2014: 138).

The other key theoretical insight that this chapter draws upon is that, not only is human agency constrained by structural limitations as highlighted above, agency is also to a very significant extent embodied and therefore unconscious. Human beings are socially predisposed to specific behaviours, certain ways of seeing the world, as well as having particular belief systems and moral foundations. This renders as deeply naïve, the 'liberal' idea of the rational choice actor who makes calculated decisions based on some optimal assessment of all the relevant facts. It also means that agency itself can be said to be structured, insofar as, it has a structural character. This makes more sense if the following statement is considered, 'we are not in fact free to be whoever we want to be, or to do whatever we want to do'.

This chapter will seek to overcome the limits of subjectivism and objectivism, (social phenomenology and social physics), in order to account for the epistemic virtues of each while at the same time skirting the vices of both (Bourdieu and Wacquant, 1992). This shall be achieved by focusing not only on each, but upon the relation between the two. By focusing on the dialectical relation between people and the worlds they inhabit, it becomes possible to account for the justifications, the shared norms and values, as well as the collective conventions that make up the eviction practices of housing professionals. In short, this relational investigation captures what neither a phenomenological account nor an objectivist critical perspective can capture, by introducing the contents of World Three, or as Bourdieu calls it, 'Objectivity of the Second Order'.

A Matter of Perception

Because the mind is a diacritical machine, it structures the world in binary form. Although this is how the architecture of the mind perceives the world, it is not how the world actually is. An example of this is evident in the famous 'two faces/one vase' optical illusion in which only one can be seen at a time. It is possible to alternate quickly between them, and it is also obvious that they are both there, but only one can be perceived at any given time because only one can become the focus of attention at any given moment. This phenomenon represents a severe limitation of the human mind and its ability to perceive the *connectedness of the things of the world*. It places the human animal at a distinct disadvantage when it comes to experiencing reality, since the universe is, as the monists of classical philosophy have pointed out, one single thing, and not the many things our minds construct in order to comprehend it.

The task of social science, therefore, is to address this deficiency, by overcoming the binary nature of human perception and thought in order to apprehend the world, as far as is possible, in its 'totality'. The challenge, taken up by many of the 20th century's social scientists, was to dissolve the false dichotomies that our diacritical minds construct in order to understand the world as it is, rather than as it appears to common sense perception. This was achieved by highlighting the importance in understanding the relational nature of reality. If, as classical philosophy suggests (from the

Figure 7.1 The face/vase illusion.

great traditions of Eastern thought, to the Monists of the ancient Classical world, and to Spinoza and beyond) the universe is one thing, which our minds divide into many things in order to perceive and make sense of it, we need to find a way of reducing the 'separateness' we create when we divide the world up. One such way of doing this is to take account of the dialectical relation between the things we dichotomise. Focusing on the dialectical relation between things reconnects that which our minds seek to separate. To say that the relations between things are dialectical is to account for the fact that each has influence over the other. They have, as Elias (see Hughes, 2008) points out, a strong degree of 'interdependence'. The example Elias uses is the chess grandmaster who, simultaneously playing multiple opponents of an inferior standard in an exhibition tournament, still has to contend with their moves, she still has to react to their strategies, while devising strategies of her own. No matter how much 'stronger' the grandmaster is, each player has a degree of control over her, just as she has over them. This notion of interdependence not only reconnects the binaries our minds create, it accounts for the 'power' and influence each has over the other.

This understanding is essential for dissolving the false dichotomies which have plagued the social sciences for centuries. The structure agency debate is one example. In order to overcome the problems that arise from our confusion over whether action is caused mainly by structural factors or by the agency of the individual, Bourdieu (1977, 1990) argues that we need to turn our attention to the relation between them. He does this through his conceptualisation of 'field' and 'habitus'. It is the product of the dialectical relation between individuals and their external world, between subjective and objective forms of reality, that Bourdieu ascribes the term 'objectivity of the second order'. This shared set of practices moves beyond the mere notion of the intersubjective which, because it exists in codified form, (that is to say, as collectively recognised within organisations, institutions and groups), represents an important, if secondary form of objective reality. These collective conventions can be said to constitute a form of objective reality because they exist independently of any one single consciousness, and have been largely 'legitimised' through 'acts of institution' thus becoming recognised as 'official'. Objectivity of the second order also represents an object of study within which it is possible to capture the relation between the individuals who make up a field and the structural possibilities and limitations offered by the field itself. In simple terms, this theoretical approach understands practice as the relation between people and the world they inhabit.

The Problem with Common Sense

The inability of the common sense view to adequately account for the exercise of power and its effects makes it blind to the fact that commonsense is, itself, a political relation, held together by categories of perception that emerge from the struggles between competing powers. In all but the most violent exchanges between competing groups, these struggles are mostly hidden behind euphemised forms of discourse and obfuscated forms of action, obscuring their latent political potency. One of the main failings of the common sense or liberal viewpoint is that, rather than questioning the 'legitimacy' of the dominant order, it promotes it, unchallenged. Thus, the commonsense view fails to acknowledge the fact that in any particular age or epoch, the dominant ideas are very rarely anything more than the ideas of the dominant. Another weakness of the common sense perspective is its inability to capture the relational nature of reality, with its tendency to see things as static, fixed, and detached. The critical view, arising from the general principle that the universe is one thing that our diacritical minds perpetually separate into fragments for the purpose of apprehension and comprehension, needs an approach that captures not how things 'are' but how they 'relate' (as 'processes' that are in constant flux, always moving, always changing) rather than states of inertia.

The relational nature of reality means that although there is much to be gained from understanding the world of housing in general, and evictions practices in particular by drawing upon objectivist and subjectivist perspectives, it provides only a partial picture of reality. To achieve as 'complete' an understanding of evictions as possible it is necessary to study not one or the other, but both together while additionally taking account of the *relation* between the two. The products of this relation, between the world and the people who inhabit it, are the conventions that make up practices, traditions, knowledges etc. It is by examining this relation that we can move beyond the limits of social physics (objectivism) and social phenomenology (subjectivism) by adding to our understanding the products that arise from the ways in which both interact.

As shown in Figure 7.2, our knowledge of the world emerges from our interaction with it. Practices arise from the relation between people and the world they inhabit.

This world is not the 'entire' world, but the very specific world that persons find themselves in. The World of Housing, as we saw in Part I of this book is located within a wider political economy that is in a constant state of flux. As the political economy is transformed through the endless struggles between competing groups, the effects are transferred to the structures of the world, evident in the way that the dominant tenure has shifted in line with the needs and requirements of the dominant means of production or capital accumulation in any given epoch. The world of housing becomes a bounded territory, governed externally by legislation, by policy, by regulation and inspection regimes. The behaviours of the people who populate this world are influenced by an assemblage of technologies, such as performance indicators, regulatory targets, inspection criteria, audit regimes, accountancy frameworks, societal expectations, all of which have the power to set or to change priorities within a specific world.

Policies and rules, however, are not simply implemented by automatons – by unthinking, unfeeling agents who merely carry out the orders they are given. For sure we cannot underestimate the power of the state to create reality through its own monopoly over the classificatory regimes that 'define' reality, but equally, as we have come to see in the evidence presented here in this book, neither can we underestimate the power of resistance that is ever present within 'fields' such as housing. The state plays an important part in defining reality as well as constructing 'subjectivity' through the

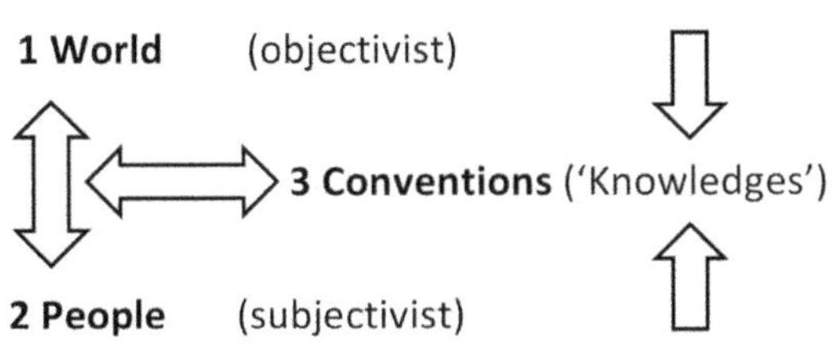

Figure 7.2 The relational model (general).

Note
The framework upon which this relational model is based, mirrors the structure of this book and is employed to explain the complex relations between housing professionals, their external economic and political environments and collective conventions, shared norms and values and common practices that govern evictions.

Figure 7.3 The relational model (as it relates to housing).

various technologies of governance it has at its disposal, but it cannot be ignored that people, particularly when organised in groups, institutions or professional fields, have a great deal of autonomy.

Figure 7.3 shows, diagrammatically, the process through which the world and the people who inhabit it, combine to form the collective conventions, the codified professional practices, the shared sets of particular norms and values that underpin evictions.

The three case-studies in Part II of the book, showed that the People of Housing (the housing professionals who participated) were undoubtedly influenced by the external world within which they were located. It was clear that housing law, the regulation and inspection regime, resource restrictions, political and economic priorities, all had a profound effect on the way that housing officers approached evictions, how they regarded third sector organisations, how they dealt with immigrants. By taking seriously the views and opinions, as the three case-studies did, it was possible to capture the illusive 'insider view', the subjectivist perspective on the objective world within which it was located. However, it does not account for the tensions, the conflicts and the contradictions that unfurled throughout the interview data.

In Case Study 1, the people of housing – with their organisational policies and procedures, their professional codes of conduct, their personal drives and ambitions – had to contend with the legislative and regulatory powers of the state. It was from this interaction, the accommodation between both, that practices arose. Eviction practices can be said to have emerged from the relation between the internal workings of the landlord organisation and the external pressure from the government and the courts. In Case Study 2, the relation was narrowed to feature the interaction of the housing professional with statutory obligations on one hand and the third sector worker whose job was to enforce tenants' rights on the other. This relation, like that in Case Study 1, was a source of great tension and conflict and resulted in the views and opinions, as well as the practices that emerged from the interview data in this case study. Similarly, in Case Study 3, the interaction of housing professionals who saw their role as providers of housing, and the politicised demands of the state to impose border control functions, also resulted in tension and conflict. This relation, between housing professionals and the punitive paternal state, shaped the forms of resistance that were evident within the interview data in Case Study 3.

What this 'dialectical' model shows is that whether or not those who populate a particular field are passively receptive to the external influence of the world, or they are resistant to it, the relation between the two is ultimately what produces knowledge, and through the collective conventions these generate, forms of professional practice. What may have become apparent, as we have journeyed through these three different, but related case-studies, is the extent to which they are awash with contradictions. What emerges from the data is the apparent ability of professionals (housing professionals) to move between positions, to take up different perspectives, depending upon the situation they find themselves in. This relational model shows that the outcomes can never be purely determined, they are never certain and therefore remain difficult to predict.

This relational model is useful for showing, in both a conceptual and diagrammatical form, how practices and knowledges emerge out of the interaction between people and the specific worlds they inhabit. What it does not do is explain why. It cannot tell us how the housing professionals who carry out evictions justify what they do, and how they bolster this justification by criticising others who do things differently. Having examined the 'world' in which housing is located, and through which evictions are governed, and having taken account of the people and their own personal, 'subjective' views on evictions, it is now necessary to explore the conventions that arise from the interactions between the two.

This begins with a word of caution. That there is a 'true' subjectivity is doubtful. A number of philosophers, particularly phenomenologists, have focused on individual experience of the world, but the idea that there is a 'subjective' experience that is unique, and entirely original to each person contains some limitations since the feelings and sensations we have, are not only mediated through the restrictive medium of language, they are also the product of an internalisation of the external world within which we have ourselves been 'socialised', of which we are, very much a product. The things we are attracted to, the things that repel us, are more instinctual than rational. They are more unconscious than conscious. They arise from the durable sets of dispositions that are instilled in us as through the long yet imperceptible process of socialisation.

Intersubjectivity arises from the process in which individuals, having a direct relationship with the world, are 'stimulated' by feelings, sensations, and moods, that arise from various situations. This is what Spinoza (1996 [1677]) called 'affects'. The process of rationalisation of these 'affects', according to exponents of contemporary social psychology, comes after we have a 'gut feeling' about something. We feel first and rationalise second. Reason, as Scottish enlightenment philosopher David Hume (2011 [1748]) points out, is always the slave of the passions.

The reactions that humans have to these affective phenomena only become intersubjective when we move from the individual to the collective phase, when in order to understand and to be understood, we have to convey these 'personal feelings' in ways that other people will understand. This is what Boltanski and Thevenot (2006) call the movement from *personal convenience to collective convention*, when an individual has to make their 'as-yet-uncategorised' feelings and thoughts intelligible to others. The best and most effective way to do this is to revert to the myriad sets of pre-agreed, well-founded, and recognised frames of reference. These frames, through which people understand the world and make themselves understood, are themselves, sets of collective conventions. In short, this process implies an initial gut feeling, deriving from the predispositions that people have acquired during their developmental stages of socialisation, followed by an attempt to make intelligible these intuitive 'gut feelings' through rationalisation, a process that is also inextricably linked to one's position in social space.

In order to try and 'show' how this process 'works', 'Moral Foundations Theory' (Haidt & Graham, 2007 and Haidt, 2013) will be utilised to capture the unconscious, infraconscious or 'innate' relation that people have to the world. Second, Boltanski and Thevenot's Economies of Worth model will be employed to capture the true extent to which people think and communicate through collectively sanctioned 'frames', that are largely determined, not upon a social background, as classical sociology would suggest, but rather on a person's specific 'situation'.

Boltanski and Thevenot's (2006) Economies of Worth model is based on the principle that the 'critical moment', the need to justify ones' self in any situation of dispute, comprises a significant part of our day-to-day social interaction with others. Indeed, not only are persons required to continually justify their actions both to themselves and to others, they are often compelled to strengthen this justification through actively criticising what others do differently. These justifications have to follow a series of rules of acceptability, something that involves the establishment of equivalence, that is to say, that persons must, in resolving these justificatory disputes, establish what they (both sides) have in common. To achieve this equivalency 'persons must divest themselves of the personal conveniences of their subjective world and converge towards a form of generality, transcending persons and the situations in which they interrelate' (Boltanski & Thevenot, 2006: 362). These ideas represent a significant development in social and psychological theory but space restrictions here preclude an adequate exposition. It is, therefore, recommended that in order to fully understand and to gain the ability to further develop this pragmatic paradigm, it is essential to read Boltanski and Thevenot's (2006) *On Justification: Economies of Worth*. In the meantime, the reader's cultural 'good-will' is required for the acceptance of the need to simplify a rather complex theoretical framework. Before doing so, it is necessary to account for justifications and justificatory regimes by tracing their origins in the pre-categorised, intuitive, unconscious realm of 'gut feelings' and their transition into common tropes that can be collectively recognised.

Moral Foundations Theory

This approach has been developed by a growing network of research psychologists in the last decade or so. It seeks to understand why morality varies so much while at the same time has so many similarities across a wide range of cultures and geographical regions. It is premised upon the fact that there exist a broad set of universal psychological systems that constitute the foundation of an intuitive ethics. Each culture then constructs virtues, narratives, and institutions on top of these foundations, thereby creating the matrix of moralities that can be observed within a wide range of cultural settings around the world. Haidt and his colleagues have identified six 'moral foundations' that their ongoing research is working to develop and refine as more data is collated and analysed.

These are represented by a set of six binaries upon which the moral world is founded, and are as follows;

1 *Care/harm* – This foundation is related to our long evolution as mammals with attachment systems and an ability to feel (and dislike) the pain of others. It underlies virtues of kindness, gentleness, and nurturance.
2 *Fairness/cheating* – This foundation is related to the evolutionary process of reciprocal altruism. It generates ideas of justice, rights, and autonomy.
3 *Loyalty/betrayal* – This foundation is related to our long history as tribal creatures able to form shifting coalitions. It underlies virtues of patriotism and self-sacrifice for the group. It is active anytime people feel that it's "one for all, and all for one."
4 *Authority/subversion* – This foundation was shaped by our long primate history of hierarchical social interactions. It underlies virtues of leadership and followership, including deference to legitimate authority and respect for traditions.
5 *Sanctity/degradation* – This foundation was shaped by the psychology of disgust and contamination. It underlies religious notions of striving to live in an elevated, less carnal, more noble way. It underlies the widespread idea that the body is a temple which can be desecrated by immoral activities and contaminants (an idea not unique to religious traditions).
6 *Liberty/oppression* – This foundation is about the feelings of reactance and resentment people feel toward those who dominate them and restrict their liberty. Its intuitions are often in tension with those of the authority foundation. The hatred of bullies and dominators motivates

people to come together, in solidarity, to oppose or take down the oppressor.

This list, the proponents of the model claim, is not exhaustive and, as they proceed with their on-going research, they are likely to expand or at least develop the categories further. These categories are included as underpinning the justificatory regimes that professionals revert to in the 'critical moment', not because there is a wholehearted belief in them, but because they represent a general framework that captures the principles of what is often latent within the unconscious and to some extent conditioned 'habitus' (see Bourdieu, 1977 and 1990). This concept of 'habitus' represents the assemblage of durable set of dispositions that human beings are endowed with, as they progress through the process of socialisation within a very particular milieu, emerging from a very specific set of socio-economic circumstances.

As a cautionary point, it has to be highlighted here that what is not being said, is that these foundations are something innate, something people are born with. The concession is a Freudian one that accepts that as humans we are part 'instinctive' and part 'socially conditioned' animals and that our unconscious drives, or 'social character' as Fromm (2001 [1941]) refers to them, constitute a significant part of what makes up our daily practices as human beings. The issue in unconditionally accepting the fact that these sets of moral foundations are innate, is made all too explicit by Foucault in the *Order of Things* (2009 [1966]) and the *Archaeology of Knowledge* (2001 [1969]) where he subjects to rigorous questioning the idea of there being such a thing as 'human nature'.

However, when translated through a social-psychological lens, moral foundations theory provides a useful means by which to account for the starting point from which the transition from personal 'subjective affects' (internal) to collective 'intersubjective conventions' (external) takes place. Moral foundations theory captures perfectly the initial 'gut reaction' a person has when confronted with a situation. A reaction that they then have to either justify, to themselves or others, and to apply some degree of critical capacity to reinforce the justification. It is this justificatory regime that will be addressed in the next section.

The Sociology of Critical Capacity

Boltanski and Thevenot's (2006) model of frame analysis is based on a number of interconnected principles. The first of these is that the 'critical moment' comprises a significant part of day-to-day social interaction. That is to say, throughout a person's normal daily life; they will be required to justify what they do. Indeed, not only are persons required to continually justify their actions both to themselves and to others, they are often compelled to strengthen this justification through actively criticising what others do differently. This 'critical capacity' is possible because humans have access to what can be called 'regimes of justification'. These regimes or 'orders of worth' are called upon when situations of dispute and compromise occur. Indeed, the interplay between these worlds or 'Economies of Worth', generate infinite matrices of conflict, compromise and collaboration.

Boltanski and Thevenot (2006) make the claim that many situations in social life can be analysed by their requirement for the justification of action. These 'regimes of justification' are mobilized within, and also transcend, specific situational contexts. What is important to note is that these regimes or orders of worth are not social worlds in the traditional sociological sense, but are rather best understood as 'discourses', 'rationalities' or 'logics'.

Adopting an approach that is arguably a development of Goffman's Frame Analysis (1986 [1974]), Boltanski and Thevenot have developed a form of 'pragmatic sociology' that captures the essence of the collective conventions that people resort to in certain situations when called upon to justify their actions. Although these conventions are collectively recognised, there is a degree of flexibility, observable in the capacity of humans to switch between different codes depending upon the situation. Switching codes is a delicate exercise that requires a degree of social dexterity and a high level of competence and agency. This ability to switch codes to suit the situation arises from the fact that individuals are limited to a collectively sanctioned set of regimes of justification and criticism. This 'limited plurality' allows people a degree of flexibility since these regimes are an integral part of their 'cultural repertoire', an assemblage of collectively agreed codes that form a kind of socially useful 'cultural tool-kit'. This 'pragmatic' approach differs from more traditional forms of critical theory in that it can be said to depend not on the social background of the individual, or on the social relations between people, but on the 'situation' that individuals finds themselves. A thorough reading of their cannon is recommended (see Boltanski and Thevenot 1999, 2006 and Boltanski 2011 and 2012), however, for the purposes of the argument made here, a very brief summary of the six regimes of worth is hereby listed:

1 *Market world* – The importance of exchange and enterprise. Prioritises competition and self-interest.
2 *Inspired world* – The importance of creativity and spirituality. Prioritises the needs of the vulnerable (child, woman, foreigner, homeless person).
3 *Domestic world* – The importance of family values and the authority of the 'father'. Prioritises hierarchy and tradition.
4 *World of renown* – The importance of Fame. Prioritises promotional activities and good public relations.
5 *Civic world* – The importance of social contracts, representation and citizenship rights. Prioritises the needs of the collective over the needs of the individual.

6 *Managerial world* (formerly the industrial world in Boltanski and Thevenot, 2006) – The Importance of productivity and efficiency. Prioritises experts and specialist professionals working effectively with systems of surveillance and control.

The 'economies of worth model' breaks from classical sociology in that it is built upon the premise that modern societies, rather than being based on a single order, have a number of interweaving orders, which are applied, not strictly on the social background of persons, but on the situation in which they find themselves having to justify something. Orders of worth can be used as justificatory regimes when the external conditions permit. Justificatory regimes are strong when they are 'pure', that is, when they do not rely on compromises with other regimes. Justificatory regimes are weakest when there is a mismatch between the regime and the situation in which it is being used.

In the broad interests of elaboration, it may be useful to apply this to the 'situation' of housing, particularly in the provision of social housing. For example, a housing officer could never justify buying and selling social housing stock for personal enrichment as the *market polity* has little influence in the narrow field of social housing provision. The universe in which markets are prioritised has no traction in the world of the housing professional. Personal gain through the profit motive is an entirely alien world to housing professionals who are tasked with the provision of essential housing services that have the welfare of tenants as their main priority. However, in the field of the private housing market, then the *market polity* will be a dominant order in the economy of worth. Similarly, a housing officer could not easily justify allocating the best social housing to those who are 'important' in the community such as community leaders or local celebrity figures, as they would struggle to justify their actions using a polity based on the *world of renown*. In fact, the privileging of family members would bring the *world of renown* and the *domestic world* into the relationship, both of which would be deemed inappropriate and could result in charges of nepotism and an abuse of power. *The inspired world* is one of the principle sources of tension between social workers, who privilege the needs of the vulnerable client (who may have addiction issues or mental health problems) and housing officers whose priority is the welfare of the entire tenant community for which they are professionally responsible (for a more detailed account of this tension see Crawford, 2015).

Some worlds or orders are very closely linked to certain areas of human activity as are the compromises that underpin their success. The Civic and Managerial worlds have combined to form the very basis of the welfare state. Indeed, Boltanski and Thevenot (1999, 2006) highlight the extent to which *the civic order* and the welfare state are dialectically linked. That is to say, a 'civic' consciousness gave rise to collectivist and welfarist policy regimes, at no time more so that during the 'so-called 'golden era' of the

Fordist-Keynesian compact (1950–1979), while at the same time these regimes developed and reinforced a sense of civic consciousness. Another polity or order of worth to emerge as a dominant ideological force from the industrial period is the managerial (or industrial) polity in which *efficiency and effectiveness* are of paramount concern. This *managerial world*, replete with experts and specialists, forms of measurement and regulatory assessment is, when combined with a strong sense of civic responsibility and pride, the perfect foundation upon which the welfare state could and indeed did, flourish.

What is not quite so clear in Boltanski and Thevenot's (2006) account but has been highlighted in other literature (Buss and Herman, 2003, Giroux, 2015 and 2019) is the link between the domestic order of worth and authoritarian (and often rightward leaning) forms of governance. The 'domestic orders'' justification of putting the family before community ('charity begins at home', 'look after your own first', 'blood is thicker than water', etc.), revering the authority of the father over that of the state, and the privileging of 'more worthy beings' (the king, the father and the boss) over less worthy beings (foreigners, strangers, women and children) has long been associated with the political 'right'. This argument will be developed further in Chapter 8. For now, it is perhaps prudent to outline the key characteristics of the four Orders of Worth that are most relevant within the field of welfare more generally and housing and evictions more specifically.

The HIGHER COMMON PRINCIPLE is that which each polity reverts to in order that 'equivalence can be maximised'. It ensures that people are *'qualified'*, qualification being the condition for assessing *objects* as well as *subjects*, determining the way in which they matter, as their value. It represents the one 'over-arching' principal under which everything else unfolds. The STATE OF WORTHINESS is that which allows people to assess the order's attachment to the 'common good'. Worthy beings are guarantors of the HIGHER COMMON PRINCIPLE, making "available the yardstick by which importance is measured" (Boltanski and Thevenot, 2006: 141). The SUBJECTS are the people (worthy or unworthy beings) who inhabit each polity and the OBJECTS are the things of that world. It is the relations between OBJECTS and SUBJECTS that help objectify the worth of persons involved. The RELATION OF WORTH is a means by which the worthy and unworthy can be separated by spelling out the way that SUBJECTS and OBJECTS contribute to the common good. The REALITY TEST is the 'peak moment' in a situation in which the outcome is uncertain. Its function is to 'test' the relevance of the relations between SUBJECTS and OBJECTS, and their contribution to the common good.

These are theoretical models and conceptual tools. The housing professionals interviewed did not identify the collective conventions under which their actions have been categorised as 'Orders of Worth' or as 'Polities'. These 'frames' do nonetheless provide a useful theoretical lens through which to understand the shared norms and values that professionals revert

Table 7.1 Economies of worth model

	Civic world	*Managerial world*	*Domestic world*	*Inspired world*
HIGHER COMMON PRINCIPLE	***The preeminence of collectives***	***Efficiency***	***Engenderment according to tradition***	***The outpouring of inspiration***
	Collective, All, Will (general)	Performance, Future	Generation, Hierarchy, Tradition	Inspiration
STATE OF WORTHINESS	***Rule-governed and representative***	***Efficient***	***Hierarchical superiority***	***Inexpressible and ethereal***
	Unitary, Legal, Rule governed, Official, Representative, Authorised, Confirmed, Free	Effective, Functional, Reliable, Operational	Benevolent, Well brought up, Wise, Distinguished, Discreet, Reserved, Trustworthy, Honest, Faithful	Bizarre, Unusual, Marvelous, Unspeakable, Disturbing, Exciting, Spontaneous, Emotional.
SUBJECTS	***Collective persons and their representatives***	***Professionals***	***Superiors and inferiors***	***Visionaries***
	Public collectives, Party, Federation, Office, Committee, Elected official, Representative, Delegate, Secretary, Member.	Expert, Specialist, Person in Charge, Operator	**More worthy beings:** Father, Kings, Ancestors, Parents, Family, Grownups, Leader, Boss **Less worthy beings:** Unmarried person, Foreigner, Woman, Child, Pet, Others, Visitor, Neighbours	Spirit, Freaks of nature, Shade, Monster, Fairy, I, Child, Woman, Madman, Artist

OBJECTS	***Legal forms*** Rights, Legislation, Decree, Order, Measure, Courts, Formality, Procedure, Transcript, Infringement, Capacity (electoral), Code, Criterion, District, Programme, Policy, Statement, Ballot, Tract, Slogan, Seat, Headquarters, Local office, Acronym, Card	***Means*** Tool, resource, Method, Task, Space, Environment, Axis, Direction, Dimension, Criterion, Definition, List, Graph, chart, Calendar, Plan, Goal, Quantity, Variable, Series, Average, Probability, Standard, Factor, Cause	***The rules of etiquette*** Good manners, Proper behaviour, Rank, Title, Dwelling, Introduction, Signature, Announcements, Gifts, Flowers.	***The waking dream*** Mind, Body, Dream, Unconscious, Drug
RELATION OF WORTH	***Relation of delegation*** Membership, Representation, Delegation, Expression (of aspirations)	***Control*** Control, Manage, Organise, Operation	***Respect and responsibility*** Authority, Subordination, Respectability, Honour, Shame	***The universal value of uniqueness*** Genius, Independent.
REALITY TEST	***Demonstration for a just cause*** Assembly, Council, Meeting, Movement, Dispute, Justice	***Trial*** Launching, Setting up, Putting to work, Achievement	***Family ceremonies*** Celebration, Birth, Death, Marriage, Social events, Conversation, Distinction, Nomination	***Vagabondage of the mind*** Adventure, Quest, Mental Voyage, Pathfinding, Lived Experience

Source: adapted from Boltanski and Thevenot, 2006.

to, when having to justify their actions or criticise the actions of others. It is this theoretical context that will inform the analysis of the data that follows in Chapters 8 and 9.

Recapitulation

The aim of this chapter was to build a theoretical model that could, in its application, make more sense of the interview data presented in Part II of the book. This chapter has made a case for a critical approach to housing studies to replace the mainstream liberal approach that currently dominates the field. Rooted in a common sense perspective, the liberal approach is limited to capturing only the superficial nature of reality, since it is blind to the fact that common sense is, itself, a political relation. Rather than question the orthodoxy of any given epoch, the mainstream view serves merely to reproduce it, unchallenged. As an entirely political construction, the common sense, liberal perspective in entirely unsuitable for the task of social scientific enquiry. What is required is an approach that can unmask the hidden forms of power and domination in ways that show the extent to which that which passes for the 'natural' and the 'necessary', are never anything more than the 'arbitrary' and 'historically contingent'.

In order to overcome the limiting distortions of the diacritical mind, a relational approach has to be developed to capture the dialectical processes that arise from the interaction of people and the worlds they inhabit. However, this is only the beginning of a more complex process. Once we accept that practices and knowledges arise when people and their worlds collide, it is possible to start the process of constructing a model that can account for the common moralities, shared normative codes and collective conventions that endow the social world with its structure and 'meaning'. In order to do this, a pragmatic approach to critical theory has been adopted, which seeks to build upon an entire assemblage of social phenomena. Based on the moral foundations of human capacity, this model seeks to account for the process in which a person moves from their individual gut feeling, their instinctual reaction to a situation, to a position in which they are able to make this moral foundation intelligible, to both themselves and others. Not only do humans have to make sense of their world and their actions within it, they have to justify these actions, in a convincing way that is difficult to simply dismiss by others.

By synthesising moral foundation theory with pragmatic sociology, in the form of Boltanski and Thevenot's Economies of Worth Model, it is possible to achieve a depth of understanding that highlights the virtues of objectivism and subjectivism while skirting the vices of both. In short, it is possible to gain access to a modality that is the product of the relation between people and their worlds, an insight that is significant for the understanding of professional practice. This significance stretches well beyond understanding the primary relation between people and world to reach the secondary relation, 'peopled worlds' and 'other peopled worlds'. As we have seen, the relationship between housing officers and tenants depends upon the relation between the tenant and their ability to pay their rent. In this respect the housing officer's world, with duties and obligations that are influenced by targets, regulations, requirements and laws, is very different from the tenant's world. When the housing officer comes into contact with the tenant-in-rent-arrears, this relation is characterised, not only by the meeting of two different people (landlord and tenant) but by the meeting of two different worlds.

Similarly, the relation between housing professionals who have duties and third sector workers who enforce these duties, is fraught with tension and conflict. This is because, although the subjects (tenants) and objects (courts and eviction decrees) are largely similar, the priorities that both sets of professional have towards them are very different. The housing professional privileges the interests of the tenant community, the third sector worker privileges the interests of their individual client. This results in two similarly structured worlds coming into conflict. More abstractly, the third case study shows the extent to which the world of the landlord or housing provider differs from that of the border guard or immigration officer. The tension arises when either one is forced to undertake the role of the other.

In summary, it takes only a slight shift in perspective, in order to create tension and conflict within worlds that, from the outside, appear similar, and that seem to share the same values, aims and objectives. By taking seriously the views and opinions of housing professionals and then subjecting them to an objectivist analysis, it is possible to gain valuable insights into the reasons why tensions exist between professional groups who may often appear to have much in common. This is the task of the remaining chapters of this book.

References

Berger P. and Luckman T. (1991 [1966]) *The Social Construction of Reality. A Treatise in the Sociology of Knowledge*. London: Penguin.

Boltanski L. (2011) *On Critique: A Sociology of Emancipation*, Cambridge: Polity.

Boltanski L. (2012) *Love and Justice as Competences*, Cambridge: Polity.

Boltanski L. and Thevenot L. (1999) 'The sociology of critical capacity'. *European Journal of Social Theory*, 2 (3): 359–377.

Boltanski L. and Thevenot L. (2006) *On Justification: Economies of Worth*, New Jersey: Princeton University Press.

Bourdieu P. (1977) *Outline of a Theory of Practice* (R. Nice, transl), vol. 16, Cambridge: Cambridge University Press.

Bourdieu P. (1990) *The Logic of Practice*, Cambridge: Polity Press.

Bourdieu P. (2014) *On the State: Lectures at the College de France 1989–1992*, Cambridge: Polity Press.

Bourdieu P. and Wacquant L. (1992) *An Invitation to Reflexive Sociology*, London: Polity.

Buss D. and Herman, D. (2003) *Globalising Family Values: The Christian Right in International Politics*, Minneapolis: University of Minnesota Press.

Crawford J. (2015) 'The (unintended) consequences of governance? Examining the role of "Frames" in creating Imaginary housing systems and their importance for understanding the practices of senior housing professionals'. *Housing Theory and Society*, 32 (3): 302–319.

Foucault M. (2009 [1966]) *The Order of Things*, London: Routledge.

Foucault M. (2011 [1969]) *The Archaeology of Knowledge*, London: Routledge.

Fromm E. (2010 [1941]) *Fear of Freedom*, London: Routledge.

Giroux H. (2015) *Dangerous Thinking in the Age of the New Authoritarianism: Critical Interventions Politics, Culture, and the Promise of Democracy*, New York: Routledge.

Giroux H. (2019) *Terror of the Unforeseen*, Los Angeles: LARB.

Goffman I. (1986 [1974]) *Frame Analysis. An Essay on the Organisation of Experience*, Boston: Northeastern University Press.

Haidt J. (2013) *The Righteous Mind: Why Good People are Divided by Politics and Religion*, London: Penguin.

Haidt J. and Graham J. (2007) 'When morality opposes justice: Conservatives have moral intuitions that liberals may not recognize'. *Social Justice Research*, 20: 98–116.

Hughes J. (2008) Norbert Elias, in R. Stones (Ed.) *Key Sociological Thinkers*, Basingstoke: Palgrave MacMillan.

Hume D. (2011 [1748]) *An Enquiry Concerning Human Understanding*, London: Simon and Brown.

Marx, K. (2003 [1894]) *Capital Volume III*, London: Pluto Press.

Popper K. (1978) *The Three Worlds: The Tanner Lecture on Human Values*, Delivered at The University of Michigan April 7, 1978, https://tannerlectures.utah.edu/_documents/a-to-z/p/popper80.pdf.

Spinoza B. (1996 [1677]) *Ethics*, London: Penguin.

8 The Parallax of Professional Practice

Exposition

This chapter will consider how to account for the tension and conflict that persists in situations in which individuals and groups appear to have shared aims and objectives, and who, all too often, are required to work in partnership, or in some form of alliance in order to further a shared objective. The contradictions that have emerged from the evidence presented in both Part I and Part II will be explored and explained in order to gain new insights into professional practice more widely and professional practice relating to evictions in particular.

Employing the theoretical model that helps us account for both the moral foundations that guide people's emotional responses as well as the frames through which these responses are made to accord with the external world within which the situation arises, helps us gain a more profound understanding of professional practice. In doing so, we will see that the relations between groups of professionals, who are often dealing with the same issues, see these issues very differently, even though the difference between what they do may only be very small. In order to grasp the contradictions that issue from these differences, a conceptual device will be employed that can account for the tensions and contradictions that can arise between two 'related' professional groups, especially when they appear to share a great deal in common.

This conceptual device will be called the 'parallax gap'. A parallax can be defined as the apparent displacement of an object caused by a change in observational perspective. The parallax of professional practice is the term used here to denote the differences that arise between practitioner groups due to the fact that, although they are dealing with the same issue (in this case evictions), they often have different priorities, which create different viewpoints. It is through examining the differences in perspective within and between professional groups that it becomes possible to capture the dialectical relations between structure and agency, field and habitus, position and disposition, from which practices emerge. Identifying and analysing the parallax of professional practice uncovers the extent to which agency and notions of practice are themselves structured. Using the tensions and contradictions between professionals engaged in eviction practices set out in the three case-studies laid out in Part II of the book, this chapter will demonstrate that the material conditions and symbolic determinations that structure the field of housing, are themselves lodged at the very heart of professional practice in housing. In short, the parallax of professional practice shows the extent to which structural factors and acts of agency are largely indistinguishable.

Let us begin by briefly revisiting what exactly the parallax is. The definition, provided by the Cambridge English Dictionary is:

> the effect by which the position of an object seems to change when it is looked at from different positions.

For our purposes, the concept of the parallax gap will be used to show that when there are different viewpoints, the shared object (tenants with rent arrears, statutory duties, borders and the imposition of new roles such as policing these borders) is seen differently in each case, depending on the perspective of the 'observer'. This method can be useful in showing the extent to which the 'distance', be it operationally, practically, or ideologically, between two sets of professionals working in the same field, can not only be measured but grasped and understood. It also accounts for the ability of professionals, in any setting, to be able to oscillate freely, without apparent contradiction, between different orders of worth, depending upon the situation they find themselves in.

Taking each case study in turn, this chapter will outline this innovative approach to understanding professional practice, through an examination of the parallax gaps that open up within the struggles between groups over the legitimate right to not only define 'social problems' but to say what should be done about them.

Case Study 1: 'I Just Want Tenants Who Will Pay Their Rent on Time'

The data from the case studies in Part II showed that a number of parallax gaps had emerged between and indeed within groups dealing with the subject of evictions. On one hand, there were the third sector agencies, and on the other, the housing professionals involved in evicting their tenants for rent arrears. The data showed that those who act on behalf of tenants make the claim that evictions make no sense on an economic or social level as they are extremely costly, cause great social harm to the household (particularly children) and often result in the household having to be re-accommodated in social housing or the more expensive private sector. Yet, as alluded to briefly in the previous chapter, by employing the Civic and Managerial orders of worth to their actions, the housing professionals interviewed could offer robust justifications for their role in evicting tenants for rent arrears.

As highlighted, the Civic order was used extensively to justify 'why' evictions were necessary and the Managerial order was used to justify the actual 'process' of evicting tenants for rent arrears. In short, if the housing professional could satisfy her/himself that their actions were in the common interests (the REALITY TEST of the Civic order) and that the arrears management process had been rigorously implemented (the REALITY TEST of the Managerial order) without success, the eviction could be entirely justified. The Managerial order privileges concerns that revolve around the 'effectiveness' and 'efficiency' of the rent collection methods (OBJECTS) and the 'experts', 'advisors', and 'professionals' (SUBJECTS) who are engaged in their 'operation' (RELATION OF WORTH). Although the Civic and Managerial orders form a useful compromise, particularly in the running of welfare services, there was evidence that one takes precedence over the other as the shift in focus changes.

Indeed, the data collected in the evictions for rent arrears case study showed the extent to which displacement can take place as a result of this shift in perspective. As the interviewees were asked about the causes of rent arrears, they were almost unanimous in their use of 'structural' as opposed to 'pathological' or individual factors. They were almost all sympathetic towards their tenants, many of whom were 'victims' of an unfair political and economic system. There is nothing surprising in this framing of the answer, since it is what would be expected, coming from a strong Civic perspective. What is interesting is how this point of view shifts to a more critical one as the broader concerns of the conversation shifts from a Civic to a Managerial focus.

What is significant is that the questions relating to the causes of rent arrears were asked at the very beginning of each interview and questions relating to alternatives to eviction asked at the end. In order of frequency the structural causes of rent arrears were: inadequacy of the benefit system, the state of the economy, unfavourable employment issues, multiple debts, cost of living increases and general deprivation. Yet, once the discussion had moved onto rent arrears management and mechanisms for obtaining rent, including legal remedies, the interviewees had all but abandoned their original perspective in favour of one that laid the blame firmly at the door of the 'irresponsible' individual. The initial answers, relating to structural causes of rent arrears were so completely displaced that by the end of the interview, questions pertaining to 'alternatives to eviction', the last to be asked, resulted in not one single interviewee believing that any viable alternative could or indeed should exist. There was complete unanimity that evictions for rent arrears formed an essential management tool for obtaining rent, even though many housing professionals had, during the interview, raised questions about their effectiveness, stating that in many cases, they simply had to write off the rent arrears, foot the expensive legal bills and meet the cost of re-letting the property.

This is the root of one such parallax gap, exposed here by a stark contradiction in the justification of evictions for rent arrears by housing professionals. The organisations representing tenants opposed evictions on the grounds that they are unnecessarily punitive, overly authoritarian and made neither economic nor social sense. Although the housing professionals tended to agree with this perspective at the beginning of the interview, by the time they had journeyed through the full range of managerial mechanisms for encouraging 'responsible' behaviour in what they had previously identified as a structural problem, they were universally unanimous in their view that evictions were entirely necessary (although some expressed this fact regretfully). The process of justification, the need to make the transition from a Civic frame to one dominated by the Managerial order of worth, caused a parallax shift in how the interviewees saw the issue of rent arrears. Two irreconcilably different perspectives on the same problem emerged, held by the same people, at different points in the discussion.

When asked about the possibility of implementing a non-evictions policy, objections were universal. They ranged from some interviewees stating that evictions were required to 'send a message out to other tenants that non-payment will not be tolerated' to the more extreme examples in which a non-eviction policy constituted a shameful abrogation of responsibility by the landlord who, by removing the threat of eviction, actively encouraged tenants to get into unsustainable levels of debt. The data showed that as the events under discussion gained more of a Managerial focus, the Civic frame was diminished. The parallax shift in perspective is always dependent on a change in the situation, one that requires a person to justify themselves.

It was evident from the data that the Civic order is used to construct a number of justificatory positions one of which places the landlord in a position of 'responsibility' (towards the 'collective' group of tenants) while at the same time critically placing the tenant with rent arrears in a position of 'irresponsible individualism' (which harms the 'collective interests' of the 'community of tenants'). The concerns of 'irresponsible individuals' not paying their 'fair share' are addressed through what appears to be a highly comprehensive array of interventions and mechanisms to both manage rent arrears and to provide advice and assistance to tenants who are in financial difficulty or economic hardship.

These Managerial mechanisms include an array of 'professionals' and 'expert advisers' (SUBJECTS) such as money advice teams, and welfare rights officers who use 'tools', 'resources' and 'methods' (OBJECTS) in their pursuit of 'effective' and 'efficient' (STATE OF WORTHINESS) levels of income maximisation that not only benefit tenants but ensure that landlords have a much higher success rate at obtaining rental payments (THE REALITY TEST). Many landlords employ their own 'in-house' money advisors and welfare rights officers in teams which operate exclusively for their own tenants, and some landlords will use local services such as Citizens Advice Scotland as well as an array of local resources such as community law centres and drop-in services.

One important aspect which appears in the data is that these interventions (and indeed much of the funding that was made available to landlords for such interventions) were all aimed at helping the tenant to cope with financial difficulty and economic hardship as well as to deal more effectively with a benefits system that was universally criticised for its inadequacy. All of this was exacerbated, according to the housing professionals who participated in the research, by increasing levels of wage-work insecurity, reduced hours and part-time working arrangements. This contradiction, related to the first, defines the second parallax gap that opens up between those who oppose evictions and those who think them entirely necessary. It can be argued that this type of 'strategic policy' redirects the focus from the causes of poverty and marginality (at a structural level) on to the tenants themselves with the interventions designed to help the tenant cope better with rising unemployment, austerity cuts to services and welfare. The explosion in new projects and services is evidence that not only is the state facilitating a shift away from its own structural deficiencies and placing responsibility onto the individual, it is creating opportunities for other sections of society, who are then enlisted into the enforcement side in what becomes a continuously rightward tilting process (Wacquant, 2012).

The data here suggests that the Managerial order is an essential means by which housing professionals can both assess their own STATE OF WORTHINESS which is determined by the relationship between SUBJECTS ('experts', and 'professionals') and their OBJECTS ('tools' and 'resources' for doing the job). The most compelling evidence for the influence of material considerations upon differences in professional practice between the two types of social landlord, was found in the answers to questions relating to 'discretion'. As Case Study 1 showed, local authority landlords were much more likely to used discretion, whereas, housing association landlords, despite there being a statutory obligation to prove that eviction was the last resort, were much more likely to make the claim that they did not operate any discretionary measures at all. This was justified by housing association professionals using the Civic frame, stressing that the most important aspect of the procedure was equivalence, i.e. treating everyone the same, irrespective of their circumstances, household, vulnerabilities. The alternative explanation, which some interviewees from local authorities gave was that simply put, discretion was widely used when the landlord had a statutory obligation to re-accommodate the household. This obviously meant that local authorities had a strong financial incentive to prevent the eviction when there would be a duty to rehouse the family; an economic pressure from which the housing association sector was spared.

What the data in the rent arrears case study shows is that an 'accommodation' between Civic and Managerial orders (which in some cases takes the form of a continual fluctuation between both), within the field of social housing provision, has resulted in a carefully constructed discourse which fosters the justification of its own practices while at the same time utilising the critical capacity which issues from the combined effects of both orders ('community of tenants' = good, 'irresponsible individual' = bad, 'effective systems' = good, 'inefficient procedures' = bad). This is what Bourdieu (1991) refers to as the sets of 'epistemological couples' which make up the categories of perception through which we make sense of, interact with and understand the social world around us.

These are the collective conventions which structure professional practice within each field, which has its own rules and strategies, its own language and logic as well as its own profits and risks which make it unique in the wider bureaucratic field. A person's position within the field is an influential factor, but it is the situation that persons find themselves in, more than the person's social characteristics or position, which largely determines the frames used. In this case, housing professionals combine elements of Civic and Managerial orders of worth for two discernable reasons. The first is the importance of rental income. For many, if not most landlord organisations, (particularly housing associations) rental income represents the most significant means by which they can fund their respective enterprises. Decades of steady erosion and in some cases eradication of various social housing subsidies has greatly lessened the ability of councils, and less so housing associations, to absorb and sustain even a low-level of accumulation of rent arrears. Second, the level of rent arrears constitutes a key performance target which is routinely scrutinised by the Scottish Housing Regulator. Indeed, as shown in Chapters 2 and 3, the encroachment on day-to-day forms of housing management practice by an increasingly regulatory approach to the financial affairs of social housing has had perhaps the greatest influence on the way 'professionalism' and 'professional practice' have developed since the dawn of the 21st century.

These two material influences arguably represent two sides of the same coin. The need to obtain rent (for the common interest) and the requirement to prove, through the system of regulation and inspection, that this is being done effectively and efficiently (as optimally as possible), create a situation that leads to an encroachment of the Managerial into the Civic order. This turns tenants into 'customers' and tenancy agreements into 'contracts', elevating arrears recovery mechanisms and prioritising interventions such as income maximisation and welfare benefits advice. It is the dialectical relationship between the objectivity of the first order, (i.e. the structural constraints embodied by austerity cuts to budgets, increasing levels of conditionality and social control, the implementation of Universal Credit and the relegation of social housing and the privileging of owner occupation) and objectivity of the second order (such as the Civic and Managerial orders of worth that professionals employ in their daily justifications) that have the most significant influence on codified forms of professional practice.

To summarise the analysis of this case study, there are different perspectives from which evictions can be viewed. Given the extent to which the views and experiences of those who are subject to, or are at threat of eviction, have been covered elsewhere (see Desmond, 2016 and Lancione, 2017a, 2017b and 2019), this study focused on the professional viewpoint, incorporating those who defend the tenants at threat of eviction and those who carry out the evictions themselves. This presents a major parallax gap. Although the two groups have broadly the same concerns, namely the rights and welfare of tenants, the different priorities represented by the tension that arises between meeting the needs of the individual against those of the community create corresponding tensions in the relations between rights-based legal advocates and housing professionals who have statutory obligations to meet. In addition to this macro level parallax gap there exists more nuanced micro level gaps that emerge from the shift in perspective within each group. This, thinner, gap appeared when the shift in perspective from a Civic to a Managerial frame was observed, manifesting in a transition from structural to individual causes of rent arrears.

The second case study provides a nuanced insight into practice, through an examination of the conflicts that arise from the irreconcilable differences embodied by the parallax gaps, which emerge from two distinctively different relations toward the 'tenant'.

Case Study 2: 'They Don't See the Bigger Picture'

The second case study highlighted the tensions between, on the one hand, the voluntary sector, whose role is to uphold the rights of tenants and to prevent, where possible, evictions for rent arrears; and on the other, the social landlord sector that evicts its tenants. As the evidence presented in Case Study 2 shows, the tension here arose from the fact that the situations in which the clients of the voluntary sector found themselves, meant that the voluntary sector workers ordinarily tend towards the Inspired Order of worth when justifying their actions and criticising those of others. The Inspired World appears to be, statistically speaking (Bourdieu et al., 1999, Boltanski and Thevenot, 1999 and 2006), an attractive order of worth for those who work in charitable and voluntary sectors with vulnerable people who exist at the edges of the social and economic spheres. It is also a feature of spiritual life, particularly those proactively involved in spiritual activism such as Quakers in the UK, or other progressive evangelical groups. This places them in direct conflict with those for whom the Civic and Managerial orders are privileged, since its foundations are largely antithetical to the rule-governed, mainstream, managerial tropes that define the official world of welfare services.

On the surface, the two sectors (voluntary/third sector and local authority/housing association) appear to have similar roles, namely ensuring the welfare of tenants, badly housed people and the homeless. They also work under the same sets of rules, regulations and laws. However, as demonstrated in Case Study 2, there is a discernable gap between both, that cannot be easily bridged. This parallax gap is founded on the simple distinction that the voluntary sector case-worker tends to prioritise the needs of their client, who is always an individual or household; while statutory housing providers regard themselves as having a responsibility for the entire community of tenants.

From the Inspired World, the advisor or caseworker representing the 'client' is predisposed to have sympathy for the chaotic substance user, the vulnerable person, the person with mental health problems, someone released from prison, the outcast or the socially unacceptable. Conversely, the drug user, the prostitute, the repeat offender, the care leaver, groups that are shunned by those who have the interests of the wider community as a central focus, are welcomed by the charitable and spiritual sectors of society. Indeed, this is the 'type' of tenant the housing professional would go to great lengths to avoid 'imposing' upon the community by providing them with accommodation. Justifying their actions from a Civic frame, the housing professional finds nothing more irresponsible than subjecting a collective of tenants in a block, a street or indeed entire neighbourhood, to someone who may pose a risk or inflict harm on the collective of ordinary, rent paying and law-abiding tenants.

For the housing professional, the case-worker, either from a charitable organisation or someone such as a social worker, is often seen in an antagonistic light, since it is their job to ensure that the rights of their clients are upheld. This often means taking the landlord to court to ensure that they adequately discharge their statutory obligations and duties. The parallax gap, in this case, is not only unbridgeable it is the source of great tension and antagonism. It arises from the practicalities of what each side has to contend with. Both sides, in representing the interests of their respective client group, believe that their actions are entirely 'fair' and wholly 'justifiable'. Furthermore, each sees her own particular perspective as the most 'righteous'. That is to say, the moral foundations that underpin these justifications, namely care/harm and fairness/cheating, can be applied to each category in different ways. For the housing officer, their duty of care is to the community, the focus being to avoid harm by placing among them someone they believe to be a 'problematic' tenant'. The charity worker sees their duty of care differently. The vulnerable individual, being largely at the mercy of the structural inequalities that perpetuate social suffering, is deserving of care. Ensuring their rights to welfare and housing is one of the most effective ways to preventing further harm. It is also easy to see how the fairness/cheating foundation is tangled up with notions of the deserving and undeserving, of care and harm, thus easy to see why both statutory and voluntary sectors would have divergent views.

Yet the parallax is never acknowledged as such. As the data shows, the process is highly euphemised, with each side in the conflict having strong justificatory frameworks for their actions. The housing professionals vociferously object to organisations representing the interests of individual tenants and the homeless, engaging in 'combative action' which often involves publicly 'naming and shaming' them (for failing in their duties). This, housing providers claim, is evidence that these organisations 'do not see the bigger picture', which is another way of saying '*they* focus on the 'individual' (which contradicts their own STATE OF WORTHINESS in the Civic world), '*we*', they claim, '*focus on the collective*' (HIGHER COMMON PRINCIPLE in the Civic world). In employing a strong Managerial frame which justifies their own actions insofar as they believe that they have done everything in their power to resolve the issue, housing professionals utilise Managerial means (OBJECTS), allowing them to insist that, procedurally speaking, a line has to be drawn somewhere. For the charitable or voluntary worker, the 'evangelical role' (HIGHER COMMON PRINCIPLE in the Inspired world) they have to adopt in legally enforcing the state's statutory obligations may be an emotional and sometimes 'disturbing' (STATE OF WORTHINESS) task, but one which is an unavoidable adventure or quest (REALITY TEST) if they are to remain 'independent' (RELATION OF WORTH) of the state, in order to uphold the rights of their 'vulnerable clients' (SUBJECTS).

The opposition between the Civic/Managerial and the Inspired world represents two different sets of justificatory frameworks, for two apparently similar sectors, who have two identical sets of SUBJECTS and apply similar sets of OBJECTS to two very different tasks. The parallax gap here provides a great deal of information, not only about the nature of professional practice, but about how social welfare services work in practice. This parallax is also vitally important for understanding how an uneven distribution of power at the level of organisations, can translate into material inequalities amongst sections of the population. Statutory providers have more 'legitimacy' and 'authority' than many if not most voluntary and third sector organisations simply because they are embedded within the state's bureaucratic function.

Case Study 3: 'They Want Us to Become Immigration Officers. It's Not Our Role'

Case Study 3 showed the extent to which housing professionals, defending the Civic nature of their role in providing housing, resisted the imposition of duties that they regarded as punitive, authoritarian and thus antithetical to how they perceived their role as landlords to be. In the third case study, the housing professionals interviewed, regarded the destructive forces of immigration rhetoric (see Peck et al., 2009, 2013 and 2017 for an introduction to the 'creative destruction' of actually existing neoliberalism) as eroding the very values upon which the Civic state was founded. The housing professional or landlord can justify evicting the tenant on the grounds of their 'irresponsible' behaviour, but this justification collapses when the housing provider is forced (by law) to evict or deny housing to someone because of their (immigration) status.

What this case study shows is that this process of creative destruction is a dialectical struggle between groups that occupy opposing sides of the classificatory divide that arises from the dual nature of the State. On the one hand, there is a persistent anti-immigration rhetoric which, advanced through much of the mainstream media in the UK, is framed around a 'Domestic polity'. This 'Domestic order of worth' promotes hierarchies (SUBJECTS – what the framework refers to as 'more worthy beings') that privilege the rule of the 'father', (the 'sovereign ruler', the 'boss', the 'manager') while relegating the role of what the Economies of Worth framework refers to as 'lesser beings', that is, 'women' and 'children', 'strangers' and 'immigrants'. This 'Domestic' order is largely an 'individualising' trope (RELATION OF WORTH) i.e. the 'family' before the 'community', 'us' before 'them', 'insiders' before 'outsiders'), actively promoting a perspective on welfare that is motivated by the need to protect scarce resources, rather than promoting the redistribution of wealth, or achieving social justice. This Domestic polity sits in opposition to the Civic order of worth, which rejects the individualising discourse of the family and family values, in favour of a broadly collectivist approach in which the 'good of the many' is promoted over that of the individual or the 'few'.

When the Civic and Managerial orders are applied to the issue of rent arrears, then it becomes much easier to justify evictions because it frames the issue around irresponsible individual 'behaviour' that, despite a raft of Managerial interventions, has caused 'harm; to the collective of tenants. Yet when faced with the authoritarian, hierarchical and often openly prejudicial tropes which come with the Domestic order, the idea of evicting individuals and households on the grounds of (immigration) 'status' rather than (irresponsible) 'behaviour' becomes much more difficult to justify and therefore largely unthinkable. As evidenced in Case Study 3, even private sector landlords and their representative organisations were opposed to the terms of the Right to Rent part of the *Immigration Act 2016*. This suggests that even when the principle feature of the private rented sector is profit, it is still largely entangled with notions of providing a public good or at least a valued service to a broad community of people who need to be housed. This is an important distinction because it shows that landlords, both social and private sector, do not object to the prescriptions of the *Immigration Act 2016* because they face extreme sanctions (up to five years in prison) for non-compliance; rather they object to them because they have invested in, through the construction of meaning, value and worth, what they do for a living. They have built up an *economy of being* that has endowed their lives with such meaning (which of course has to be constructed) to the extent that they cannot simply walk away from it, easily give it up or lightly surrender it to the political whims of those who have appropriated the institutions of the state.

It is this very source of meaning that leads to parallax gaps opening up within practice, in this case between those who work in the field of housing and those who work in the authoritarian sectors of the state. The driver of this parallax gap is the *rightward tilting* of the bureaucratic field. This is broadly defined as the imposition of the punitive functions of the state's right hand onto the welfare functions of its left hand. The bureaucratic assemblage is a key component of the wider assemblage of power, which constitutes the State. In this paradigm, the state is not a unitary monolith of governance, which, headed by a 'ruling class', serves the interests of a specific group. It is, rather, an arena within which various groups, entangled in a network of *co-operative competition*, struggle for the monopoly over the legitimate right to define issues, such as social problems, the solutions to which arise from the process of selecting which problems warrant recognition and which are ignored.

Bourdieu's innovative conceptualisation of the bureaucratic field, is structured around the notion that the 'left hand' of the state is perceived as the nurturing side, which is responsible for the welfare of its citizens. The left hand of the state is responsible for health care, education, social housing, welfare, etc. The 'right hand' of the state is made up of the disciplining institutions, which, by contrast, police, control punish and incarcerate. Both the left hand and the right hand exist in antagonistic cooperation (since they occupy different positions within the bureaucratic field, and therefore have differently corresponding political outlooks as well as being driven by differently corresponding internal logics). The rightward tilting of the state is what Bourdieu (1994, 1998, 2003) refers to in explaining his observations of the increasing intrusions by disciplining institutions in issues and problems that would have previously been reserved to interventions by the left hand. As mentioned in Chapter Three, the dual effects of both privatisation and increasing levels of 'regulation' and 'inspection' have had a longstanding effect on public services in the UK (see Raco, 2016), a fact that has resulted in services being run according to business models while at the same time being much more proactive in promoting policies with surveillance and the modification of behaviour as a principle objective.

Following on from the previous chapter, there are moral foundations that embody the Leviathan, a creature, with two hands (see Hobbes, 2016 [1651]), one caring and nurturing and the other disciplining and punishing. The care/harm and fairness/cheating foundations are the primary emotions that underpin the Civic Order of Worth. Care and the avoidance of harm, or at least policy innovations that reduce harm are bound together with a sense of justice that has notions of fairness and cheating at their core. The authoritarian/subversion and loyalty/betrayal foundations that manifest through the Domestic Order of Worth are at the very heart of the state's right hand. In the UK (as well as with Trump in the US) in recent times, the political manifestations of these very foundations have been shrouded in claims that they border on, or at least touch upon, ideological tropes that are at their base, characteristic of the far right. Similarly, as Virdee and McGeever (2017) argue, the campaign to take the UK out of the European Union had a strong undercurrent of racism, coupled with the desire to back control of the UK's borders.

In relation to Case Study 3, the complex entanglement of binary positions, moral foundations and collective conventions can present something of an opaque and rather difficult-to-grasp conceptualisation. In an attempt to make the relational and dichotomous nature of this model more accessible, a diagrammatical representation has been created that highlights the main facets of each category.

Wacquant's (2009) analysis shows that this shift from the left to the right hand of the State, has resulted in the double regulation of those who are at the periphery of the economic sphere, that is, those who are situated in the precarious regions of the lower strata of social space. This is not to suggest that the left hand of the bureaucratic Leviathan is an entirely benign force; indeed, Wacquant (2008, 2009) acknowledges the seminal work of Fox Piven and Cloward (1971) in uncovering the ways in which welfare regimes provide the state with additional means by which to regulate and control marginalised groups.

The civil tensions and unease created by unemployment and austerity, unfurling through 'disciplinary supervision over the precarious fractions of the post-industrial proletariat' (Wacquant, 2009: 307), creates a behaviour changing welfare system, a work-enforcing benefit system, a rent enforcing social housing system, as well as a debt enforcing credit system (see Lazzarato, 2013, 2015 for evidence of the latter). All of which are configured to modify behaviours and to foster the surveillance of 'risky' groups. In the context of this study on immigration controls, particularly with regard to housing, this 'rightward' tilting of the State promotes a regime, which in cases such as the implementation of the Right to Rent, prioritises

Figure 8.1 The left hand/right hand of the State.

'status' crimes over crimes of conduct (Malloch, 2016). Nowhere is this shift more visible than in the binary forms of categorisation that emerge from the wide range of oppositions, which govern the practices of landlords. These sets of inescapably cognitive and evaluative presuppositions:

> paradoxically unite those whom they divide, since agents have to share a common acceptance of them in order to fight over them or through them, and so to produce position takings which are immediately recognised as pertinent and meaningful by the very agents whom they oppose and who are opposed to them.
>
> (Wacquant, 2005: 100)

It is within this governing tension, between the left and right hands of the state, that the binary oppositions (such as those who are either 'deserving or undeserving' of assistance, who are 'citizens or non-citizens', 'genuine or bogus' asylum seekers, 'real or fake' victims of trafficking, 'legal or illegal' immigrants) are legitimised and in turn prioritised by institutions of the state. What the data from this last case study shows, is that the binary oppositions and the governing tensions, from which they arise, create the forms of discrimination that force open a parallax gap between the government and the social housing sector in both Scotland and England.

Thus, we come full circle. The dialectical relation between institutions of the state vying for the legitimate right to define social problems and their solutions has brought us back to the diacritical nature of perception and the irreconcilable differences it produces. Professionalism cannot be understood beyond the parallax nature of practices.

Grasping reality in a non-linear way is difficult, due to the mind's diacritical urge to organise the world in binary form. It is perhaps easier if we think relationally, taking the mental concepts that we construct as being enmeshed into one another. It is perhaps best to think about these concepts as being, like people and the world they inhabit, dialectically linked. Moral foundations provide the immediate 'gut reaction' a person has to a situation, but these gut reactions are also socially conditioned. Someone who grows up in a social environment where 'good manners' are important and the 'practical' is privileged over the 'ideal', when the 'real' is preferred to 'fantasy' or 'wishful thinking', when family obligations are prioritised over 'freedom' to do as one wishes, rather than as one ought, these persons will be predisposed to what Adorno et al. (1950) called the 'Authoritarian Personality'.

By leaving unquestioned and unchallenged, the taken-for-granted norms presented by orthodoxy, then the problems underlying the (mis)recognition of the current failures in our social welfare setting, the constant tensions and contradictions that emerge from the practices of street level bureaucrats across the entire sector, will forever remain masked, obfuscated and euphemized by *interests* that are aligned to the maintenance of the status quo. This idea will be developed in the next chapter.

Table 8.1 The moral, worth and parallax matrix

Moral foundations	*Economy of worth*	*Political parallax gap*
Care/harm: This foundation underlies virtues of kindness, gentleness, and nurturance. **Fairness/cheating:** This foundation generates ideas of justice, rights, and autonomy.	**Civic world:** The importance of ***social contracts, representation and citizenship rights.*** Prioritises the needs of the collective over the needs of the individual.	**The left hand of the State** • This is the communitarian world of cooperation, embraced by progressives it represents the foundations of the welfare state. • *It is opposed by those on the authoritarian right as the 'nanny-state' for interfering in and thus limiting human potential.*
	Inspired World: The importance of ***creativity and spirituality.*** Prioritises the needs of the vulnerable (child, woman, foreigner, homeless person).	• This is the world of artists, activists and spiritual people who seek 'enlightenment and emancipation'. • *'Realists' and 'practical' people reject it as an 'airy-fairy', unrealistic world that privileges the needs of losers and dropouts, over the righteous and hardworking.*
Loyalty/betrayal: This foundation underlies virtues of patriotism and self-sacrifice for the group. It is active anytime people feel that it's "one for all, and all for one." **Authority/subversion:** This foundation underlies virtues of leadership and followership, including deference to legitimate authority and respect for traditions.	**Managerial world:** The Importance of ***productivity and efficiency.*** Prioritises experts and specialist professionals working effectively with systems of surveillance and control.	• This productive world view is inhabited by a wide range of social groups from civic organisations to corporations, the politically partisan and proponents of brand loyalty.

(*Continued*)

Table 8.1 Continued

Moral foundations	*Economy of worth*	*Political parallax gap*
		• *Managerialism has become such a dominant political trope that only those from subcultures beyond the mainstream are overtly critical of it.*
	Domestic world: The importance of ***family values and the authority of the 'father'.*** Prioritises hierarchy and tradition.	**The right hand of the State** • This is the closed and exclusionary world of authoritarian traditionalism that privileges family values and authoritarianism. It also tends to oppose immigration and favours oppressive and punitive policies of surveillance and control. • *It is rejected as harmful by the creative classes, the progressive political left as well as some spiritual communities.*

References

Adorno T., Frenkel-Brunswik E., Levison D. and Sanford R. (1950) *The Authoritarian Personality*, New York: Harper and Row.

Boltanski L. and Thevenot L. (1999) 'The sociology of critical capacity'. *European Journal of Social Theory*, 2 (3): 359–377.

Boltanski L. and Thevenot L. (2006) *On Justification: Economies of Worth*, New Jersey: Princeton University Press.

Bourdieu P. (1991) *Language and Symbolic Power*, Cambridge: Polity Press.

Bourdieu P. (1994) 'Rethinking the state: The genesis of the bureaucratic field'. *Sociological Theory*, 12 (1): 1–18.

Bourdieu P. (1998) *Practical Reason: On the Theory of Action*, Cambridge: Polity.

Bourdieu P. et al. (1999) *Weight of the World*, Cambridge: Polity.

Bourdieu P. (2003) *Firing Back: Against the Tyranny of the Market*, London: Verso.

Desmond M. (2016) *Evictions: Poverty and Profit in the American City*, London: Penguin.

Fox Piven, F. and Cloward R. (1971) *Regulating the Poor: The Functions of Modern Welfare*, New York: Pantheon.

Hobbes T. (2016 [1651]) *Leviathan*, London: Penguin.

Lancione M. (2017a) 'A început ploaia/It started raining: Fighting for the right to housing in Bucharest'. https://vimeo.com/205064103.

Lancione M. (2017b) 'Revitalising the uncanny: Challenging inertia in the struggle against forced evictions'. *Environment and Planning D: Society and Space*, 35 (6): 1012–1032.

Lancione M. (2019) 'The politics of embodied urban precarity: Roma people and the fight for housing in Bucharest'. *Geoforum*, 101: 182–191.

Lazzarato M. (2013) *The Making of Indebted Man*, Chicago: Semiotext(e).

Lazzarato M. (2015) *Governing by Debt*, Chicago: Semiotext(e).

Malloch M. (2016) 'Criminalising victims of human trafficking: State responses and punitive practices', in M. Malloch and P. Rigby (Eds), *Human Trafficking: The Complexities of Exploitation*, Edinburgh University Press, Edinburgh.

Peck J., Brenner, N. and Theodore, N. (2017) 'Actually existing neoliberalism', in D. Cahill, M. Cooper, M. Konings and D. Primrose (Eds), *The Sage Handbook of Neoliberalism*, Sage, London.

Peck J., Theodore N. and Brenner, N. (2009) 'Post neoliberalism and its malcontents'. *Antipode*, 41 (S1): 94–116.

Peck J., Theodore, N. and Brenner, N. (2013) 'Neoliberal urbanism redux?' *International Journal of Urban and Regional Research*, 37 (3): 1091–1099.

Raco M. (2016) *State-led Privatisation and the Demise of the Democratic State: Welfare Reform and Localism in an Era of Regulatory Capitalism*, London: Routledge.

Virdee S. and McGeever B. (2017) 'Racism, crisis, Brexit'. *Ethnic and Racial Studies*, 41: 1802–1819.

Wacquant L. (2005) *Pierre Bourdieu and Democratic Politics*, Cambridge: Polity Press.

Wacquant L. (2008) *Urban Outcasts: A Comparative Sociology of Advanced Marginality*, Cambridge: Polity.

Wacquant L. (2009) *Punishing the Poor: The Neoliberal Government of Social Insecurity*, Durham: Duke University Press.

Wacquant L. (2012) 'Three steps towards an anthropology of actually existing neoliberalism'. *Social Anthropology*, 19 (4) 66–79.

9 Power, Housing and Politics

Exposition

Having constructed a theoretical model and then applied it to the case study evidence in the previous chapter, some valuable insights emerged in respect of professional practice. One of these insights revolved around the notion of a parallax gap, a shift in perspective that is both the cause and effect of a change in priorities, out of which arises tension and conflict between worlds that often appear to have in common the same subjects and objects. It also reveals the extent to which the relationship between the 'situation' (the insider view) and the material circumstances (the external world) has a profound effect on how people see and interpret the world of which they have an active part in and of which they are a product. This model is useful in that it is not limited to an understanding of professional practice in housing or evictions, since it can be usefully employed in most, if not all areas of professional practice and in an equally wide number of professional fields.

First, through the forensic examination of a particularly insightful answer to a question given by a Chief Housing Officer in Case Study 1, it will become evident that 'professional competence' implies the ability to seamlessly oscillate between two 'compromise' frames in order to create a robust and credible justificatory framework. Second, in an act of epistemic reflexivity, I will highlight the extent to which the 'subjectivist' perspective is limited in understanding what people do and why they do it. Third, in direct reference to the interview data from the Chief Housing Officer and from my own experience, this chapter will explore one of the most profoundly hidden aspects of professional practice, the issue of 'interest'. By using the 'game' analogy favoured by phenomenologists (see Schutz, 1972, [1932] and Merleau-Ponty, 2002 [1945]), this chapter will show the extent to which the 'game' (the professional field and the symbolic profits over which professionals compete) remains hidden or at least obfuscated by the players (in this case housing professionals) themselves. One of the most insightful aspects of professional practice is the universal denial of the very fact that the 'game' is a game, with a range of very specific symbolic profits representing the rewards for success. The *symbolic profits* which include the various forms of recognition such as 'prestige', 'status', 'standing' 'reputation', and other esteem indicators such as 'awards', 'promotions', 'secondments' are always augmented when done under the guise of 'selflessness', 'personal sacrifice', and 'hard work'.

In returning to the first of these three insights, Case Study 1 will be briefly revisited in order to show, empirically, the links between 'professional competence', especially at a senior managerial level, and the ability to oscillate freely between orders of worth in constructing a robust justification of professional practice.

Development

The following two excerpts are from the Chief Housing Officer of a large local authority. The data presented here is an answer to a question (that I, the interviewer put to the interviewee) of fairness. In the interests of reflexivity, it would have to be acknowledged that this question was a provocative one, which arose from my own sense of injustice. This was based on my own perception that one rule existed for social housing tenants (and welfare recipients more generally) while another rule existed for global economic elites. The reasoning behind this assertion was that the latter group were able to mobilise teams of accountants and lawyers to take advantage of a wide range of accounting loopholes and offshore secrecy jurisdictions in order to avoid paying tax on both wealth and heritable property transactions. At the same time, social tenants were held accountable and routinely punished for every single penny they could not afford to pay. The answer given by the Chief Housing Officer is an example of exactly how professional competence, the product and the producer of successful careers in state bureaucratic institutions, represents an important dimension in understanding the role of orders of worth (frames), in justifying professional practice.

Excerpt 1[1]

> No, there was an issue of *fairness*, there was an issue of a *collective* here, whose service is provided in a very particular way and everybody has to accept their *responsibility* within that. But actually, I would rationalise it in a much cruder way. Housing is not a complicated activity and it revolves around a very simple document which is the tenancy agreement. Now we've turned the tenancy agreement into a 35 page event, at its core it's a very simple agreement and it is that *the tenant will live in the house, not damage it, not annoy the neighbours* and pay their rent, and in return for that we will protect their occupancy, maintain the condition of that property and a wider range of services at local government context, improve that house and keep it to a particular standard, *and defend their peaceful occupation against*

> *those who would disturb it, so we will deal with their neighbours if their neighbours - tenant or not - seek to harass them or disturb them in their home.* And that's the deal, it's a very simple one but it's a contract for services and if you do not pay for the service you are receiving then there is no other service – and I will have that conversation – I will say that to tenants, 'help me out here, you've effectively not paid, you owe us £2,500, that's a year's rent, go through the bills that you have in your head, so you've got a phone, you've got TV, you've got gas, you've got electricity, how many of those services would you still be receiving a year after you last paid for them? And the answer is in every single case absolutely none, the house is no different, you have to understand this is something you need to pay for'.

Excerpt 1 is striking as it begins with three of the key concepts central to the creation of a Civic frame; namely 'fairness', the 'collective' and 'individual responsibility'. Then the interviewee switches to a Managerial order, focusing on the contractual nature of the tenancy. The fact that such a 'simple document' has been made into a '35-page event' is itself indicative of an attempt to 'managerialise' something that previously existed to inform the tenant of their rights and responsibilities as prescribed by the relevant pieces of housing legislation. This 'managerial' process of turning a simple tenancy agreement into a detailed contract transforms the landlord tenant relation into one in which the former creates a mechanism for managing tenant behaviour (see also Dean, 2000, Flint, 2009, McKee, 2009b, Manzi 2010, Jacobs and Manzi, 2019b). Combining both Civic and Managerial orders allows the Chief Housing Officer to justify the council's position on evictions while at the same time allowing for a degree of critical capacity to be levelled at the tenant who 'does not stick to their end of the deal'. The conversation continues thus, adding more interchangeable justifications and criticisms within frames that interchangeably correspond to these justifications as the discourse develops.

Excerpt 2

> but in the meantime, my job's to get the rent in. If I don't get the rent in I can't deliver a service. *Every one of our tenants signed an agreement, they said 'I'm going to live in this house and I'm going to pay the rent' ... they signed an agreement.* Now in any world, it does not matter what system that world is run under, people can reasonably be expected to be held to account for the agreements they reach and the promises that they make, and people can also reasonably expect to have to pay for the services they receive. It is as simple as that. *So the bottom line is that paying your rent is an obligation that you take on, it's a social obligation, it's an obligation you make to other tenants*

> effectively and if you don't make it explicit that, 'rent is needed to pay for this service', you know, then *if you don't pay your rent somebody else is paying it for you.* We do not constrain our investment programme because of our rent arrears, we do not limit repairs because of the rent arrears, the only sanction you will get is that where you were entitled to a declaration allowance, for example, a cash payment to help you after capital works, basically we put that to your rent arrears instead of giving it to you in money, and that's it, *so if you're still getting the service and you're not paying for it, that is not acceptable, you're taking money from your neighbours' pockets* and I put that in front of folk. I mean, I deal with all the other highfaluting stuff around that if you like, but this is the real problem.

Excerpt 2 highlights a number of interrelated points. First, this is a very 'specific' response, drawing upon an entire repertoire of Civic and Managerial tropes. The Chief Housing Officer shows the extent to which the external priorities and the target driven nature of regulatory capitalism informs, and both conscious and unconscious levels, the narratives that make housing practice justifiable. There is no question that people are in the world, but what must also be acknowledged is the extent to which the world (the professional world of collective convention) is also in *them.*

Second, this dialectical relation between the individual and their world is reflected in the extent to which professionals can, depending upon their experience and position within the field, move seamlessly and to good effect, between frames of justification in ways that maximise their 'professional competence'. This 'professional competence' is, to borrow a Bourdieusian (2000) concept, a form of *institutional capital*. It represents one of the most significant forms of symbolic profit that any professional field has to offer. The evidence in Case Study 1, and in particular the excerpt highlighted above, shows the extent to which this justificatory regime represents both a 'stake' and a 'weapon' in the struggle over the acquisition of *institutional capital*. Again, the relationship here is a dialectical one. The acquisition of professional competence facilitates the accumulation of *institutional capital*, and this accumulation in turn augments professional competence. It must be noted that, the requisite levels of competence that are required to enter the 'game' in the first place, are not evenly distributed among its 'players'. The social and economic background of a person, the school they went to, the opportunities they enjoyed, the cultural capital they acquired, be it in the form of artistic ability, musicianship, literacy skills, linguistic competence etc., all provide a source of 'advantage' in the game. This advantage is, in almost every game, and at almost every level, hidden under notions such as 'dedication', 'natural talent', 'hard work' and other meritocratic mythologies. Indeed, what is most often hidden or flatly denied within professional fields, is the very fact that the game is a game, with a range of very specific symbolic profits representing the rewards for success.

One of the thematic veins that stretches rhizomatically through this book is the point that the common sense, mainstream, liberal perspective is entirely inadequate when required to unearth and expose the hidden aspects of power, particularly when it takes on a symbolic dimension. This brings us to perhaps the most deeply hidden dimension of practice, namely; the notion of 'interest'. It is said to be the most deeply hidden dimension of practice because it is 'invisible' to common sense perception, hence why it is so important to have an alternative to the mainstream liberal approach to the study of housing and the wider world of social scientific research.

Challenging the 'common sense' view of the world has been a central tenet of critical enquiry since the late medieval period (at least since the publication of Machiavelli's *The Prince* in 1532) where there was general acknowledgement that the social world that presents itself is most often illusory, leading Pascal (1670, see Bourdieu, 2000) to assert that there exists, among persons, a propensity to hide the true motives of their actions through 'performance' in order to appear *disinterested,* irrespective of the level of 'commitment' in the struggle over the appropriation of forms of capital. Drawing on the 'game analogy' made popular by the phenomenologists such as Schutz and Merleau-Ponty, Bourdieu (1977, 1990, 1991, 1998, 2000) develops the notion of *'disinterestedness'* as the masking, by the 'players' in the 'game', of the fact that there is a struggle over the stakes (forms of capital) of the game. This fundamental belief in the game, and the value of the symbolic profits that the game provides, are referred to in the Bourdieusian canon as *'illusio'*.

In fact, one could go as far as saying that Bourdieu's general metatheoretical account of what is in effect an *'economy of practices'* (Brubaker, 1985) or an *'economy of being'* (Hage, 2000), empirically informed and theoretically rich, shows that although practice is often regulated by self-interested strategies and tacit calculations, this 'objective truth', is not acknowledged by the participants, who hold to the *sincere fiction* of a *disinterested exchange*. The important aspect of Bourdieu's metatheory is that self-interest, in this economy of being, cannot be simply reduced to material interests, but rather encompasses the full range of symbolic as well as material goods. What is important to note about this, mostly unconscious, 'disposition' is that it is oriented towards seeking the kinds of 'recognition' and 'justification' that only the positive regard of others can bring (Bourdieu, 2000). This social anthropology provides the foundation of a theory of practice that acknowledges the ways in which agents, at the critical moment of a situation (the moment of disagreement), move towards 'collective conventions' in order to justify their own positions. This will be developed soon, but first a reflexive account in the form of participant objectivation, in the first person, as if I, the researcher, was participating in the research itself.

Reflections: 'I Thought I Was Che Guevarra ...'

Shortly after I transitioned from the world of front-line practice to the world of academia, I entered a new 'social universe' with its own specific conventions, its own language and sets of practices. It was both exciting and daunting. I quickly realised that the field of housing studies is split into two broad camps. On the one side there is the quantitative, policy-based world where economics and statistical analyses are the dominant methods of enquiry. On the other, there is the qualitative, theoretically informed world where a more conceptual and 'critical' approach is favoured. I was naturally drawn towards the latter camp. This camp had everything I could ever want from professional life. It had the most interesting journal articles, the most radical perspectives, Foucault, a mistrust of statistical evidence, the most interesting seminar papers, more Foucault, a healthy disregard for authority of all kinds, a scepticism towards liberals of all shapes, a refusal to engage with the 'corporate university', difficult to read books, even more difficult to write lectures and a very good social scene, the pub being the central arena for discussion, support and debate. As I got lost in this world, the 'stuff' of the other world dissolved without me even noticing. The sentiments endured but the practicalities changed. I was now working 'with' housing professionals, rather than 'against' them. Without realising it I was going through a period of transformation and then one day, I caught myself saying something that was so uncharacteristically conciliatory that I had to look around, lest there be people from my old world in the vicinity to hear and thus condemn my words. This process was accompanied by a terrible fear that I was selling out, that I'd gone soft, that my new status as an academic had removed me from the material conditions that made 'caring' about evictions, poverty and all the other social injustices, the principal and enduring concern of my life.

In order to compensate, I wrote exam questions highlighting the very worst practices, drawing on the most sensationally brutal and cruel cases that I could remember. In my housing law classes, I picked examples on account of their shock value. This approach had very limited success, so I swiftly changed tack, a process that in turn changed me in a thoroughly dialectical fashion. Before you could say 'scholastic bias' I had, myself, awoken to the fact that all was not as it had once seemed. Having ploughed my way through some difficult to read, and even more difficult to understand books, it began to dawn on me that the story I had constructed, the character I had created, the roles I had 'performed', were not quite as 'authentic' as they had once seemed.

These things rarely happen overnight. For me, it happened incrementally, and day-by-day, the façade began to dissolve. Then one morning, sitting in my room, overlooking the snow-covered campus of the picturesque University of Stirling, I realised that rather than being the 'people's champion', the Che Guevarra of housing, I was more akin to Homer Simpson, wearing a Che Guevarra T-Shirt.

Doh!

It suddenly dawned on me that I wasn't the rebel I thought I was, fighting the system, winning countless victories against the cruel and vindictive state. I was a central pillar of the rent collection function. Here was I, labouring (hard) under the illusion that I was the embodiment of resistance, when I had actually been incorporated into the very system that I thought I was fighting against.

The more I thought about it, the clearer it became, to the point where I found it hard to see how I could have possibly missed it. I mean ... looking back ... it's obvious. Clients would turn up at the Housing Aid Centre, having been sent by the housing officer from the council or the housing association, tearfully holding their eviction notice in their hand, and I would proudly 'come to the rescue'. I was so caught up in the excitement and bravado associated with stopping last minute evictions, that I was blinded to the fact that a significant percentage of my cases, particularly in the last few years of my tenure, were most probably orchestrated by housing professionals. They knew that by sending the tenant along to Shelter, we would not only stop the eviction but we would, as they say, 'lay it on the line', thick. 'Now listen very carefully'... I would say solemnly, before going to great lengths to tell them that this was their last chance, that I could not recall the decree again, that if they failed to stick to the payment plan agreed, then it was curtains. Nothing more I could do. Minutes for recall of the decree for eviction could be lodged but once. [Laughs] Here was I, thinking I was doing my clients a favour. I thought I was saving the world. Even now, when I look back at the interview data in Case Study 1, just over one third of housing professionals were in favour of the lodging, on behalf of tenants, minutes for recall of eviction decrees. Look at the data and you'll see the extent to which landlords 'the one's I had believed to be progressive and far sighted' had seconded welfare rights officers, benefits advisors, income maximisation officers, court workers, community law centres, local charities ... and me.

All it took was for a small percentage of these to refer their clients and I was run off my feet, scudding up and down the Broomielaw on my bike, running the gauntlet of inequality, serving minutes on Sheriff officers. Sure, some housing officers were angry that I'd intervened, but these are the ones I remember. Others weren't.

It wasn't until I was musing leisurely in my ivory tower at the University that I realised that I wasn't a rebel at all, I was an integral part of the rent collection protocol of every landlord who was smart enough to realise my potential as an effective assistant in their own system of rent arrears management. I was a central pillar in the rent arrears collection system. I was as much a part of the state's social control function as the Sheriffs who granted decrees, as the police who ignored illegal evictions, as the civil servants who issued guidance on how to implement the government's 'hostile environment for immigrants' policy. And to some extent, so too are a large number of welfare benefits officers, court advisors, community lawyers, income maximisation officers.... Their contribution is of the very highest value, they help to boost people's meagre income, they improve the lives of those at the margins, they stave off a whole range of unpleasant outcomes. But, at the very end of the day, we have all been incorporated. We're all part of the system.

What this kind of epistemic reflexivity shows is that the parallax gap is not restricted to relations between persons and groups. It can emerge from a shift in perspective at an internalised and individual level, through a change in focus that results in the emergence of a different set of priorities. In order to fully understand how and why this occurs, it is necessary to unmask another hidden truth of professional practice; namely the propensity of people to disguise their own naked self-interest through the almost universal performance of a disinterested exchange. One way to grasp this is to account for the fact that people, particularly professionals working in the great bureaucratic institutions, reap the material and symbolic profits on offer, by pretending, to themselves and others, that they are acting – completely selflessly – in the common interest. In fact, what is imperative to note, as Pascal did in the 17th century, is that the most valuable personal symbolic profits can be maximised, the more it seems that the efforts deployed in their attainment are done exclusively in the name of the greater good.

The weakness of the subjectivist viewpoint is that, since it is bound up in the game through the struggles over the symbolic profits on offer by the game, it is blind to the processes in which humans hide from themselves and others, their own naked self-interest in the 'game'. This is not to portray society as an assemblage of greedy and selfish individuals, acting only in their own narrow interests. Quite the opposite. What is being suggested here is that people perform a wide range of altruistic acts, because the appearance of selflessness is one of the factors in augmenting the value of the symbolic capital that can be reaped through the performance of 'disinterest'.

'Professionalism': A Disinterested Interest

Fields (professional worlds), being relatively autonomous, and thus having their own internal logic, common language, and forms of capital, are sites of competition between those who seek to either transform or conserve the structures of the field (as well as the external world within which it is located) in accordance with their own dispositions and particular interests. This interest that individuals have, in any particular 'game', varies in accordance with the material and symbolic profits each game (field) has to offer. This interest in the game, what Bourdieu (2000) calls *illusio*, is an investment in the 'game' itself, that which makes it worth playing, worth the effort. The fact that each field has its own entrance fee, either a set of skills, an array of credentials or formal qualifications specific to that field, means that those outside its boundaries are, as well as being excluded from playing, often blinded to the stakes on offer.

A useful analogy is the casual observer walking past the offices of a well-known organisation. This casual passer-bye will see people inside busily working, getting on with their jobs, the roles they have been assigned, the subjectivities they have adopted and made their own. The observer will have an idea of what the organisation does, and might even have an idea of how the working practices of those inside the offices will be structured. But what the observer won't know, with any degree of certainty is, 'what it is like'. Because of this 'distance' they are separated from the things that matter in that particular world, the things that make that world go round. It might be numbers, it might be people, money, artistic or creative capital. The casual observer is cut off from the internal politics, the alliances and allegiances, the rivalries and the competitions that make up the 'economy of being' in any professional field. The casual observer will be blind to the codified conventions that determine the divisions of labour, the priorities that determine who does what, who is in line for promotion, who has missed their targets, who are the rising stars, who are the 'one's to watch' (for both positive and negative reasons), etc. The 'experiences' that give meaning to the mundane tasks of the everyday 'work' environment are entirely human. This is why, in the interests of robust research, it is imperative to take seriously the views and opinions of professionals. But it is also important to note the limitations of this 'insider' perspective, to take stock of the fact that compared to a more objectivist standpoint, it may not be the best way to uncover the most deeply hidden structures that govern the social universe.

The insider view provided by the subjectivist perspective is essential in determining the stakes of any particular game, but it becomes limited when it is acknowledged that the players in the game themselves are predisposed to obfuscate, not only the rules under which the game is played, but also the stakes in the game as well as their own particular strategies for playing. Each professional field is a relatively autonomous space with its own internal logic, unique language and its own codified set of collective conventions. But what all professional fields have in common is the fact that they are populated by individuals, all of whom are caught up in the game (they are 'taken in' by it) and who are, proportionate to their objective 'chances' in the game, engaged in the appropriation of the game's symbolic profits, be they recognition, prestige, status, or merely just some form of acknowledgment. What all fields share in common is the fact that the strategies that are employed will almost always represent, to some degree or other, self-interested action disguised as some form of disinterested exchange.

It is perhaps prudent to acknowledge the fact that although the symbolic profits on offer within the bureaucratic field are founded upon disinterested practices such as, self-sacrifice, devotion to the common good, dedication to public service, etc., for some (particularly those who can be said to pursue career ambitions), these disinterested practices mask a deep rooted set of 'personal' interests.

> Without doubt the social universes within which disinterestedness is the official norm are not necessarily governed throughout by disinterestedness: behind the appearance of piety, virtue, disinterestedness, there are subtle, camouflaged interests; the bureaucrat is not just the servant of the state, he is also the one who puts the state at his service.
>
> (Bourdieu, 1987: 87)

Bourdieu's (2000) notion of *illusio* accounts for the stakes of the game which the agent invests in and from which the agent derives meaning (manifesting as identity, social role, status etc.), and does so by rejecting outright, the idea that agents tend to work solely for monetary gain. What is being suggested here is that agents, in this case housing professionals, seek some form of meaning in their work, through for example, fostering a sense of purpose which arises from the appropriation of the symbolic profits associated with professional engagement in 'good work'.[2] The satisfaction derived in part from the recognition given by others for performing a role which certain groups see as 'worthy', provides an added sense of value to the job and by extension, a person's life. It is this symbolic dimension which is the key to understanding, not only the ways in which housing professionals understand their world and make it meaningful, but also for understanding the correspondence between the objective (material structures) and subjective (bodily dispositions, including categories of perception) that appear to be the most natural account of the world that exists (and therefore 'right, 'correct', 'obvious').

Not only is there a compromise between Civic and Managerial orders of worth within the practices of housing professionals, there is also a compromise which takes place within the field itself. Housing professional can either 'take advantage of the possibilities the field offers, in order to satisfy their drives and desires, or the field uses their drives and desires for its own ends by forcing them to subject or sublimate themselves in order to adapt to the structures and the ends that are immanent within them' (Bourdieu, 2000: 165). As Bourdieu goes on to argue, both are observed in what becomes something of a compromise, the extent to which each is dominant or dominated, being largely dependent upon the dispositions of the 'person' and the 'professional field' within which they are located.

The same principles apply to the third sector worker or activist. The Civic World plays as significant a part, being rooted in the rights and responsibilities of civilians and local authorities, albeit with a different emphasis that sees a shift in favour of the 'individual'. The Managerial world is replaced by the world of the Inspired, where the central character is the outcast, the artist, the crazy woman, the stranger etc. To the extent that the Civic/Managerial order creates a conformity in which the dominant order is accepted as both 'natural' and 'necessary', the Civic/Inspired world fosters a sense of resistance to the dominant order. There is a tacit acknowledgement among many activists and third sector workers that the dominant ideas, as Marx had famously pointed out are, in every epoch, the ideas of the dominant, those who dominate the political economy and who have appropriated the institutions of the state. Therefore, it can be said that for some third sector workers and activists, the social problems caused by persistent levels of inequality and injustice, can be resolved through radical action that seeks to challenge the dominant world view on how goods should be distributed and who should be the main beneficiaries of these policies. In a practical sense, this entails sticking one's neck out, challenging authority, standing up for the weak and the vulnerable, being difficult to deal with and otherwise causing maximum disruption to the oppressive structures of the state. These are the traits that generate and amplify the symbolic profits most favourable to the activist or third sector worker.

Recapitulation: Beyond Utilitarianism

The arguments and analyses presented in this chapter weaken the utilitarian conceptualisation of professional practice, since it is clear, that the transparency that underpins notions of rationality and choice, are mostly illusory. Both the hidden dimensions of practice, those that are invisible even to the players themselves, and the strategic attempts of players to mask their intentions under a cloak of benevolence, meritocracy or nature, render as obsolete, the utilitarian approach to understanding the world. There are two fundamental flaws in the utilitarian perspective on 'action'.

First, that the utilitarian approach has to pretend that 'agents are moved by conscious reasons, as if they consciously posed the objectives of their action and acted in such a way as to obtain the maximum efficacy with the least cost' (Bourdieu 1998: 79). The second problem which the utilitarian position presents is that it tends to 'reduce everything that can motivate people to material benefit, economic interest, or monetary profit'.

Instead of there being conscious calculation on the part of the individual, Bourdieu (1990, 1991, 1998) claims that the relationship between the individual and the social world, consists of an infraconscious, infralinguistic complicity in which actors, through practice, constantly pursue 'goals', 'aims' and 'objectives which are never posed as such. Although the objectivist position sees clear 'ends' in the practices of others, the third parties themselves are rarely if ever consciously aware of them. Those who have developed a 'feel for the game', those who have embodied the gamut of practical schemes of perception and appreciation relevant to the field, do not need to pose the objectives of their practice as ends. From a perspective that draws on the phenomenological literature, social agents are not *subjects* faced with an *object* (or a problem) in a cognitive sense, rather they are so absorbed by the world in which they are immersed, that the 'end' perceived by the objectivist view as a 'project', is for the player, 'inscribed in the present of the game' (Bourdieu, 1998: 80).

If ever there was evidence of the importance of a 'critical' approach to understanding the social world, this aspect of practice is surely one of the most compelling. It is evident from this analysis that a great deal of the social world is hidden, from individuals absorbed in the game, as well as the so-called 'objective' gaze of those looking in. It becomes possible to increase our understanding of the social world and the human practices that bring it to life, if we can account for the relation between the two on a number of levels, in a range of modalities. Excerpt 1 in this chapter showed the extent to which professional competence and a highly developed ability to seamlessly segue between modes of justification exist proportionately to each other. This is something that the 'common sense' 'mainstream', and 'liberal' perspective misses completely. Perhaps the biggest weakness of the common sense perspective lies, not only in the fact that common sense is itself a political relation as mentioned previously, but that it masks its own naked self-interest by cloaking its activities with a vail of disinterestedness.

Like the experienced Chief Housing Officer in Excerpt 1 above, or the as-yet-unreflexive Housing Aid Worker in Chapter 1, being 'taken in by the world' within which one operates and through which one augments one's symbolic profits, distorts the true nature of professional practice, both for the practitioner, and the observer. This extends beyond the world of the housing professional to encompass almost all professional fields, none more so than the field of housing studies and that of academic research.

Notes

1 Key – if the section is in bold italics it is representative of the Civic order. All other underlined sections (not italicised) are reflective of a Managerial order.

2 When I was previously involved in the recruitment of students for the Housing Diploma, a full time professional housing qualification, it was not unusual, when at interview that the answer to the question 'why do you want to work in social housing', was framed around the notion of public service, of 'giving something back to the community', and by doing so, working in a profession that gives 'job satisfaction'. Many if not most interviewees gave reasons that I now recognise as being structured by notions which are firmly rooted in the Civic order of worth.

References

Bourdieu P. (1977) *Outline of a Theory of Practice* [R. Nice, transl], vol. 16, Cambridge: Cambridge University Press.

Bourdieu P. (1987) 'The force of law: Toward a sociology of the juridical field'. *Hastings Law Journal*, *38* (1): 805–853.

Bourdieu P. (1990) *The Logic of Practice*, Cambridge: Polity Press.

Bourdieu P. (1991) *Language and Symbolic Power*, Cambridge: Polity Press.

Bourdieu P. (1998) *Practical Reason: On the Theory of Action*, Cambridge: Polity.

Bourdieu P. (2000) *Pascallian Meditations*, London: Polity Press.

Brubaker R. (1985) 'Rethinking classical theory: The sociological vision of Pierre Bourdieu'. *Theory and Society*, *14* (6): 745–775.

Dean H. (2000) 'Managing risk by controlling behaviour: social security administration and the erosion of welfare citizenship', in P. Taylor-Gooby (Ed.) *Risk, Trust and Welfare*, Basingstoke: St. Martin's Press.

Flint J. (2009) 'Subversive subjects and conditional, earned and denied citizenship', in M. Barnes and D. Prior (Eds) *Subversive Citizens – Power, Agency and Resistance in Public Services*, Bristol: Policy Press (pp. 83–98).

Hage G. (2000) *White Nation: Fantasies of White Supremacy in a Multicultural Society*, London: Routledge.

Jacobs K. and Manzi T. (2019b) 'Neoliberalism as entrepreneurial governmentality: Contradictions and dissonance within contemporary English housing associations'. *Housing Studies*. https://doi.org/10.1080/02673037.2019.1617411.

Manzi T. (2010) 'Promoting responsibility, shaping behaviour: housing management, mixed communities and the construction of citizenship'. *Housing Studies* *25* (1): 5–19.

McKee K. (2009b) 'The "responsible" tenant and the problem of apathy', *Social Policy and Society* *8* (1): 25–36.

Merleau-Ponty M. (2002 [1945]) *Phenomenology of Perception*, Abingdon: Routledge Classics.

Schutz A. (1972 [1932]) *The Phenomenology of the Social World, Seattle*: Northwest University Press.

10 What Are the Alternatives to Eviction?

Introduction

It was not the aim of this book to produce a set of recommendations regarding evictions and eviction practices. It does not make any suggestions as to the kinds of policy interventions that work and those that do not. There will be no proposed hierarchy of groups that should receive priority treatment. No innovative proposal as to how professional groups can 'better' work together. No requests for joined-up thinking, or calls for collaborative working. You will be disappointed if you were expecting a list of good-practice examples, or any kind of engagement with the cottage industry that has been built around the 'what works' agenda. Not only would such engagement with mainstream, liberal, common sense 'solutions' represent a betrayal of the book's critical approach, it would, according to the very logic of the research findings and their analysis presented here, be completely and utterly futile. For that reason, all notions of tinkering with policies, or tweaking the legislative framework that offers protections for vulnerable groups, will be rigorously avoided.

One of the rhizomatic themes that links the three parts of this book is characterised by the 'relational' nature of an 'interconnected' world. In understanding evictions, it is imperative to understand the extent to which power, housing and politics are also inextricably linked, connecting both the macro and micro levels. Power exists in the concentration of capitals (material and symbolic) that gives the state the monopoly over the authority to define the world, to pass laws, to set priorities, to make policy and to regulate. Power exists at the micro level in that housing professionals can decide the fate of their tenants through the exercise (or not) of discretion. Behind the 'power' that the housing professional exercises, is the state itself. The laws and regulations, the pre-action requirements, the court procedures and the decrees, the Sheriffs and Sheriff Officers all lend legitimacy to a set of practices that have evolved through the interaction between the people of housing and the needs of the political economy.

This chapter concludes the book by looking at the long-term efforts of one local authority councillor to make evictions a thing of the past.

More accurately, this chapter will examine the almost universal opposition of the housing professionals towards a non-eviction policy, seeking answers to why such hostility exists.

Exposition

The journey informed this book began in 2000 when I took up employment as a Housing Aid Worker for the charity Shelter. The work for this book, particularly the research on evictions for rent arrears, began and ended with two interviews that took place a decade apart. These interviews were with a local authority councillor who was, at the time of the first interview, the Housing Portfolio Holder for his local authority. Just over ten years ago, the councillor led the push to pass a council directive that made his the first Local Authority in the UK to adopt a non-eviction policy for rent arrears. Shelter quickly linked in with the innovation, promoting it far and wide as the best solution to what they saw as an unsustainable and counterproductive practice.

At the first interview in 2010, the councillor explained to me how he had attended a surgery one day to find that a number of tearful tenants had come to see him because they had been issued with eviction notices for rent arrears. A lifelong socialist, the councillor thought this to be highly irresponsible of the council, and being the housing portfolio holder, with responsibility for both tenants, council policy and practice in housing, decided to take action. He discussed cases with the housing professionals concerned and set about the task of gathering as much information as possible. He commissioned a cost benefit analysis, the result of which shocked his fellow councillors, who were astonished by the fact that that not only did the evictions themselves not make any sense, they came at an unreasonably high cost both to the council and to the households concerned. These facts allowed him to convince all but the elected members from the Conservative Party, to agree on the passing of the non-eviction policy for rent arrears. As a result of a number of warnings from the housing managers that the policy would lead to a sharp spike in the non-payment of rent, it was agreed that the level of arrears would be monitored and the success of the policy be based on the arrears remaining at a manageable level. The policy was short-lived. The first six-month review did indeed indicate a sharp rise in arrears and the non-eviction policy was removed. Soon afterwards, a whistle blower made contact to disclose that the arrears levels had been manipulated for political reasons and that the elected members of the council had been wilfully misled. Independent auditors Scott-Moncrieff were commissioned to investigate. The investigation concluded that the relevant information had been irretrievably deleted from the system, and that it was therefore impossible to confirm whether or not the councils rent arrears had indeed increased or whether the council had been misled. Despite the suspicions that arose from this, the local authority continued with their policy of evicting tenants, albeit with an added compromise agreement to work closely with Shelter. This involved extra council staff to make enforce protocols and ensure that eviction was a last resort.

When I signed the contract to write this book, I contacted the councillor and asked if we could meet again, some ten years on, to discuss the current state of affairs regarding evictions. We were both dismayed that a decade later, we were still discussing evictions, but it did seem that the initial policy had had some positive effects. Although he said that there had been only about ten evictions in his local authority in 2019, it was, as far as he was concerned, ten too many. The hidden factor was that, for every eviction, a great deal many more went through the court process, with the vast majority prevented at some stage before the forced removal of the tenant. Indeed, the councillor talked about a current case where he managed to get the family members of one tenant to make payments, thus staving off the eviction planned for two days hence. This still represents an issue since, although the number of evictions carried out is low, the number of initial actions raised is considerably higher.

In addition to the sums of money that are spent sending letters, doing home visits, initiating court proceedings, instructing lawyers, settling legal bills and other practicalities, the cost of evictions still remain disproportionately high. The councillor said:

> We did a best value audit of a number of evictions recently at the council. There was one case where a woman had a disabled kid, and she herself had learning difficulties. The best value audit showed that that this single case alone, where they were evicted for £3000 rent arrears, cost this council roughly £70,000. It just doesn't make any sense.

What immediately impressed me was the fact that he had not given up on his vision of a local authority landlord that did not evict tenants for rent arrears. He had not been crushed under the weight of opposition and apathy. The reality, however, was that despite his determination to make evictions a thing of the past, and even with the vocal support of groups like Shelter, he faced almost universal opposition. He faced opposition from the housing professionals, and their managers, as well as from many elected members of the council. Add to this a reluctance on the part of ministers of his government and their civil servants to challenge the 'evictions orthodoxy', and what we appear to have is something of an immutable situation.

Can We Make Evictions a Thing of the Past?

In order to conclude our exploration into evictions and eviction practices, it is necessary to examine the plight of the councillor and his quest to make evictions for rent arrears a thing of the past. In doing so, we need to return to the theoretical model that was developed in Chapter Seven. This is a relational model designed to capture the dialectical nature of the world. It asserts that practice and knowledge arise from the dialectical relation between people and the worlds they inhabit. Although the diagram shows that the political economy is at the top of the box, and moral foundations are at the bottom, the box is 'one' thing in a 'monist' sense. This is because the world is one thing (more accurately, as Spinoza suggested, the universe is one thing). Our minds are limited to seeing many things, and many worlds, so this is a conceptual tool, to help overcome the mind's limited ability to perceive the world as a totality.

The World of Housing, as explored in Part I of this book, is the product of a political economy that is dominated by 'regulation' and 'rent'. At the macro level, the privileging of regulation and rent has a profound effect upon the shape and structure of the entire housing system, including the market, which is never a 'free market', but rather, is at all times a market created and promoted by the institutions of the state. This also includes the private rental market and the short-term holiday let market. Lastly, the state also has regulatory oversight of the social rented market. But it would be a mistake to think that at the macro level, the political economy is 'controlled' by a homogenous 'ruling class', a single, unified group of people. The state is an assemblage of institutions all with competing interests, all struggling for material but also symbolic resources. Boltanski

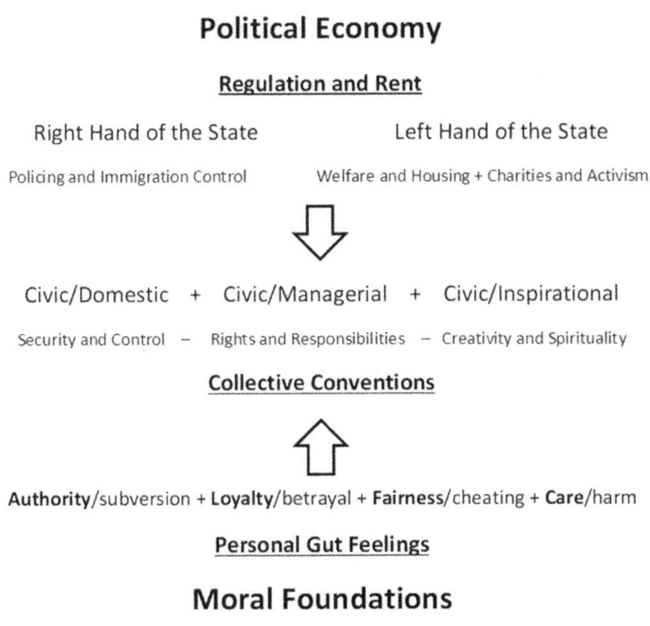

Figure 10.1 The field of housing, a relational model.

and Thevenot (2006) claim that the struggles over the appropriation of capital, have a tendency to not only produce conflict and compromise, but also collaboration, as individuals and groups seek the help and support of others who are on 'their side', to form an alliance that will improve both their chances in the game. Beyond these temporal collaborations, the groups can very easily find themselves returning to a state of conflict, or of seeking compromise.

For competing institutions and the people who strive within them, the ultimate prize is the monopoly over the legitimate right to 'define' the world, to say what things are, and what they mean. This symbolic power is at the very heart of material power, since it has significant influence over the categories of perception that structure 'common sense'. It has the ability to make the 'arbitrary' seem 'natural' and the 'contingent' seem 'necessary'. Ultimately, it is the power to universalise a particular word view. To make the view of the few, the view of the many. These struggles, in which the stakes are various types of capital on offer as well as the forms of recognition their accumulation brings, take place at both the macro and micro levels, where conflicts play out, compromises are reached and collaborations are formed. The 'game', however, does not take place on an even playing field. Not all groups have the same legitimacy, not all individuals have the same authority, not all opinions share the same 'validity'. The power structures of the state and its bureaucratic field (its left and right hands) are configured in such a way that the 'particular' view of those who make up certain groups becomes 'universalised', bound up with 'common sense', accepted as 'legitimate'.

This is the very core of the problem that the councillor had and indeed still has, in convincing people of the merits of a case that, on so many levels, appears eminently sensible. The issue has a strong degree of clarity when the 'common good' is framed as that which benefits the council (it saves money), as well as the 'community of tenants' (it is their rents that are spent on evictions) and the households themselves (these are vulnerable people, there are children who will suffer etc.). The combination of economic and social justifications makes a very compelling case for the non-eviction of tenants for rent arrears. It explains why after commissioning a cost benefit analysis on evictions the councillor was able to convince all but the Conservative members of the council, that a non-evictions policy made sense.

The Personal is Political and the Political is Personal

What the councillor perhaps did not anticipate when first he proposed the non-eviction policy, was the strength of collective resistance from the housing professionals themselves. On the one hand, the councillor had a strong case that made perfect sense from his perspective. On the other hand, the housing professionals, because of the practical demands of their role in the prioritisation of rent, were unable to see its merits. Confusion arose because the *fuzzy logic of practical sense* (Bourdieu, 1977, 1990, 2000) masks the political dimension of professional practice. The moral foundations from which justifications arise are universal, but they are not universally applied to the same objects of the world.

In the interests of clarity, the moral foundations that guide our reasoning and the frames that make this reasoning intelligible and communicable, are thoroughly political. The housing officers and the councillor who was calling for the non-eviction policy, were all in possession of the same moral foundations. They all 'cared' and wanted to prevent 'harm', they all wanted 'fairness' to prevail over 'cheating', they all wanted to remain loyal to those to whom they had a professional responsibility. What is clear is that despite having the same universal set of moral foundations, people still disagree, tensions arise and conflict ensues. The parallax gap opens up because the predispositions that people have towards the world are entirely 'political'. The political has a personal (subjective) dimension.

To 'care' is to care about something. To be loyal, is to be loyal towards something (an institution or brand etc.) or someone (a leader or figure of authority, a family member etc.). The very idea of fairness asks 'fairness of what?' (policy, the law, resource distribution?). The same goes for cheating. Some groups will see welfare benefit recipients as cheating the system by shirking their responsibility and avoiding work. Others may be entirely sympathetic to this group, holding that the tax-avoiding, offshoring, low-wage paying billionaire class are the real cheats in society. Moral foundations always exist, but the key questions are not about their existence they concern how they arise, in what context are they stimulated, who are they relevant for, who do they apply to. This represents the twofold political character of morality. This is what shapes and gives structure to the foundations and justificatory regimes that sets the councillor and the housing professionals of his local authority apart. They both have the same care/harm and fairness/cheating foundations, but they apply them differently. This difference, created by a displacement of the subjects and objects of the world of housing (tenants and rent arrears) against a background (the different priorities set in the context of the care/harm and fairness/cheating foundations and the corresponding Civic order of worth), represents the parallax gap that separates the councillor's non-eviction policy and the almost universal resistance of housing professionals.

This resistance arose from the fact that although they inhabit the same world, the Civic world of local authority housing provision, and had the same subjects (tenants) and objects (houses, policies, regulations) their relation to each of these was very different. These relations are therefore inescapably political. They are social relations, but they are also relations of power. Although they both wanted the same things (better housing conditions, fairer policies, more efficient and effective services etc.) both the councillor and the housing professionals who opposed his non-evictions policy prioritised these differently. In other words, the weight that each received, was, between the two parties, distributed unevenly. This has a subjective dimension, but more importantly, it is subject to objective or external pressures. What emerged from the interaction between people, their feelings and emotions and the structural opportunities and limitations imposed by the world was a series of meanings, desires and ultimately, practices. These practices were the product of the relation between the external world and the sets of dispositions that people had towards certain things.

It is easy to see why the councillor's colleagues from the Conservative Party would disagree with him, since they would, given their political affiliations, be statistically more likely to be from an entirely different social milieu. Occupying positions in social space that imply distance will tend to generate beliefs and opinions that are also perceived as distant. Indeed, the councillor himself is explicitly clear about his own political perspective, and why it is so:

> I come from a mining background. My family were all miners, socialists right to the core, and you never forget these values. The minute you forget these values, you'd be as well giving up politics. I have big fights in my (council) group and we need to make compromises, but the day you give up your principles, is the day you should retire from political life.

To contextualise this statement, the councillor was confused as to why housing officers and even the housing managers, people from roughly the same town and mining villages as himself, could have such different views on evictions. He struggled with the idea that fellow members of the 'working class' could justify evicting tenants for rent arrears. This level of confusion was very similar to my own when I worked for Shelter, and, although I do not come from a mining background, I grew up in a very working-class community, in social housing, and therefore share a great deal of sympathy with the councillor's vision of a better world, devoid of evictions. As evidenced in the chapters of this book, the political dimension of the world extends beyond class and settles somewhere in between social background and the situation in which people find themselves, with a number of factors privileging the significance of the latter over the former. Few factors are as compelling in determining how a person views their world, what perspective they have to adopt, what position to take, than those that accompany the necessities implied in the 'subjectivities' that arise from the position adopted when one embodies the term 'professionalism'.

This is what sets the councillor, and the housing professionals at odds with each other. Basically, they have different games to play with different rules, and different stakes. The people of the microcosm of the housing world have to interact with the rules as set in the macro-level of the political economy, rules that ultimately determine the priorities of the housing system. The combination of being under the constant regulatory gaze of the state's inspection regime, and the financial imperatives to keep arrears down, combined with the 'duty' that housing professionals adopt in protecting the interests of the wider community of tenants, has a significant effect on professional practice within the field. This is of course rooted in the 'affective' responses to events in the world. The fairness/cheating 'affect' is stimulated when housing professionals consider non-rent paying tenants to be taking advantage of those 'responsible' tenants who pay, regularly, and on time: 'Why should some be made to pay, when others refuse?' The care/harm moral foundation is stimulated by the need to not only protect the community of tenants from the 'irresponsible' actions of the few, but to protect the overall service that social landlords provide, by ensuring rent is paid, and provision is adequately funded. Not only do these narratives have political as well as moral foundations, it can be said that both the political and the moral are inextricably linked. The housing professional's position 'towards' the tenant with rent arrears takes on a moral character precisely because it has a political character. This can be seen in any professional field, evidenced by the various collective conventions that give rise to dichotomies such as 'deserving' and 'undeserving'.

The political can therefore be said to be deeply personal and the personal can be said to be thoroughly political. The political reality here is that the housing professionals are bound by the requirements of the regulation and inspection regime, lest they be subject to the oversight and sanctions that non-compliance with government policy entails. If they do not play the game, according to the state sanctioned, authorised and legitimate rules, they will find it difficult to reap the symbolic profits that the game has to offer. Other than 'mavericks' or those who self-identify as 'rebels' within an organisation, who profit from their open rejection of the game and its rules, it is difficult to accumulate the types of capital that will bestow esteem indicators such as status and reputation upon a player in the game, allowing them to move through the levels, in the quest for promotion, seniority and power within the organisation. Professionals in any field, housing being no exception, are bound by the game's rules, both tacit and official, for a number of reasons, ambition to succeed within the profession, being but one.

The councillor who envisages a world without evictions, on the other hand, is bound by no such limitations. He has a duty to both the council and its constituents. He is, to use a local saying, 'very much his own man' in this respect. He is free to resist the regulation and inspection regime and therefore free to resist the highly political character of housing policy and practice, to act, not in the interest of the landlord organisation, or the individual interests of its employees, but in the interests of his own constituents, the local authority's tenants. In short, he is free to dedicate his care and attention to helping the very people he is elected to serve. This is the Civic order of worth in its purist form, without the contamination of any Managerial compromise. My own history, as a third sector practitioner and activist-cum-academic researcher, makes me much more inclined to side with the councillor than with the housing professionals. It is easy for me to take the moral high ground and to criticise those who refuse to see the 'sense' of a non-eviction policy for rent arrears, simply because I am not bound by the professional limitations that are enforced through the regulation and inspection regime. I, too, am playing a different game, with different stakes. I get different forms of 'recognition' for playing the game differently. If they were to adopt my critical perspective, housing professionals would be subjected to the negative consequences that befall those who are deemed to be disloyal, troublesome or rebellious.

Returning to the question, how can we make evictions a thing of the past, the answer it seems, is no clearer. A person's view of eviction depends upon their position in the game, relative to the game's objectives, its stakes and symbolic profits. This is a thoroughly political situation, since these things themselves are determined, to some extent at least, by the state and its institutions, entities that are always and at all times appropriated by specific groups, to serve particular interests while giving the general impression that they are serving the universal interests of everyone. Thus, housing professionals are caught up in a practice regime that is largely, but not exclusively, determined by a regulatory system that enforces the prioritisation of rent. The housing system itself is part of a bureaucratic field that is tilting ever rightward, compelling housing professionals to adopt practices that involve increased levels of surveillance and control, as well as being actual border guards, a role that they are struggling with, but managing, for the meantime at least, to resist.

Rather than submitting to a situation in which the parallax of professional practice is an obstacle to progress, it might be more advantageous to use the parallax gap as an opportunity to open up new possibilities for change.

Parallax and Paradigm

A valuable understanding of the problem of the parallax gap was developed in 18th century by Immanuel Kant through his philosophical work on opposing positions and perspectives. Kant argued that it was not enough to see things from one's own viewpoint, or from the viewpoint of others, but to face the reality that is exposed through difference (parallax). As the parallax gap opens, so too does an entire range of new political opportunities. This chapter has shown the extent to which 'emotions' or 'affects' are political insofar as they relate to the things of the world in a socially mediated way. The process of socialisation endows humans with durable yet flexible predispositions towards things. To a certain extent it is true that we do create our own reality, but we do not do so under the social conditions of our choosing. The transition from 'gut feeling' to rational explanation entails more social processes as people search for frames that others will not only understand, but through which they will agree and ultimately support. As people interact with their world, beliefs are formed, norms are forged, collective conventions are assembled and practices emerge.

The evidence presented in this book suggests that a shift (however slight) in a person's relation to the subject (the tenant) and the object (the house that needs to be paid for in rent) can result in the opening up of a parallax gap. If, by embracing the parallax we stop trying to see the issue from both sides, and focus on the irreducible antinomy itself, it becomes obvious that the issue is not about how much rent, or how much subsidy, who should pay and who should be exempt, what punishment should there be (if any) and how should it be administered, to whom, where, and under what circumstances but more simply, about rent itself. The parallax brings into sharp focus the very idea of rent as a concept. By focusing on 'rent', rather than the practices surrounding its collection, and the management of issues around non-payment, it becomes obvious that the solution to evictions for rent arrears, is the abolition of rent.

However revolutionary, or radical this sounds, it is not a new concept. The idea of Universal Basic Services (UBS) has been around for a few years. It has emerged from the requirement to tackle a range of social, economic and environmental crises including the current climate emergency and the need to move to a de-carbonised economy, the threat to jobs posed by automation and technological advancement, as well as the challenges of an aging population due to advancements in medicine and biotechnologies. UBS constitutes a new paradigm. Given that this book has shown that practice arises from the relations between the political economy and the people who interact with it, then any change at the macro level, will have a profound impact on practice. The multiple crises that are a direct result of our current economic and political system have not only stimulated a great deal of debate, they have, in light of what has been perceived by some as a global emergency, been moved to take action. This has involved certain groups exploring alternatives to the current carbon-based model of accumulation, resulting is a shift away from the obsession with growth altogether. One of the consequences of this line of inquiry is UBS.

The Institute of Global Prosperity defines the three components of UBS thus:

> In this context, 'services' are collectively generated activities that serve the public interest, 'basic' means essential and sufficient, rather than minimal, enabling people to meet their needs, and 'universal' means that everyone is entitled to services that meet their needs, regardless of ability to pay.

In response to what it sees as the 'housing crisis', which constitutes diminishing stock, and rising rents and a general lack of affordability, particularly for young people, the Institute for Global Prosperity, based at University College London, propose that housing should join health and education in becoming a universal basic service, free to all, at the point of use. Their plan is a compelling one and is aimed at addressing a wide range of social and economic problems, the existence of which, is an indication that all is not well in the economy of the fifth richest country in the world. Their model is based on a paradigm shift in economic thinking, away from standard models of growth and the regulatory capture of rent, towards new ways of spending in order to reduce the cost of living while at the same time increasing the quality of life for the majority of people. Their fully costed plan for housing involves a significant increase in social rented stock available to tenants at zero rent.

> We model doubling the existing social housing stock by funding the building of 1.5 million new social housing units using 30-year Treasuries at current market rates. The new units would be offered on a needs basis at zero rent. All social housing would be exempted from Council Tax, and include a utilities allowance. With a 7-year building schedule the costs start at £6.1bn and finalise at £13bn from the 7th year onwards.
> (IGP 2017)

In Bastani's (2019) manifesto, what he calls Fully Automated Luxury Communism, the 'free' provision of Universal Basic Services (UBS) is central to his idea of a new political economy. Suggesting five key services that will make up the core of his UBS model, Bastani names transport, education, healthcare, information and, of course, free housing. What he is proposing is not Soviet style housing for all, where the population lives in uniform monolithic towers, rather an integrated system in which everyone's basic housing needs are met. This in no way suggests that the market be abolished, but it is set to significantly reduce housing market speculation and the environmental damage caused by insufficiently insulated housing built cheaply for maximum profit. Those who have the money and the desire for a more luxurious abode than the minimum requirement allows, are free to buy such a dwelling on the open market. As well as offering a better quality of life for many more people, Bastani's manifesto is a solution to the multiple crises that have been spawned by the excesses of capital accumulation. The idea of UBS comes at a time of potential transition in the global political economy. These innovations may seem far off but they are perhaps a little closer than we think. We not only live in uncertain times, the climate emergency, the crisis that overshadows all other crises, presents something of a stark choice for humanity. In all its simplicity it is either capitalism or planet. We can choose to continue with our carbon-based growth model or we can choose to sustain organic life on earth. We cannot sustain both.

This gives rise to a range of possibilities, with the potential to succeed where previous 'ideological attempts' to change the social, political and economic structures of the world had previously failed.

Hope for such radical change springs from the fact that the inertia that bound the first 20 years of the 21st century to the destructive confinement of actually existing neoliberalism, may not have the secure future it seemed to enjoy even a decade ago. For Fisher (2009), Capitalist Realism was the dystopic realisation that it was easier for humans to imagine the end of the world, than it was to image an alternative to capitalism. Ten years on and recent events have meant that the 'actually existing' end of the world scenario seems more 'real' than it did a decade ago. The level of change required to break the stranglehold of neoliberal capitalism also has the added advantage of not being weighed down by utopian expectation. Rather than being an 'ideological' vision that can be countered by competing ideologies, the emergence of UBS may arise from absolute necessity and be implemented by the very people who neither want nor believe in it, but who know at least, that there really is no alternative if life on earth is to be sustained.

For Bastani (2019), the current revolution in technology, what he calls the Third Disruption, has the potential to provide the solution to the multiple crises of capitalism's long and damaging legacy. This new technological age has not only the potential to replace capitalism as the dominant global economic model, but will constitute a paradigm shift that will have as much impact as the transition humans made some 12,000 years ago from hunter-gathers to famers, or indeed, the industrial revolution. The coming of the 5G network, a revolution in connectivity with previously unimaginable internet speed, will have a profound impact on the very structure of society. This unprecedented advancement will, among other innovations, herald the arrival of autonomous vehicles, changing the face of transport as well as making a significant population of professional drivers entirely redundant. It is not only drivers and manual worker's whose jobs are at risk from technological advancement, it will affect traditional professions as well. Artificial Intelligence (AI) is now advancing at such a pace that a number of traditional professions such as lawyers, accountants and even doctors will, in the next decade or so, be replaced with computer programmes that are so advanced they will be able to provide comprehensive legal advice on complicated cases, perform accountancy operations such as tax returns and book-keeping, and make diagnoses based on genetic information and developments in medical science. Bastani's manifesto suggests that rather than being a disaster, the Third Disruption could be the very thing that saves us.

A Green New Future for Housing

As alluded to at the beginning of this chapter, it is was never the intention of this book to develop a list of alternative ways of dealing with evictions.

The aim was simply to provide a more nuanced understanding of evictions by focusing on the practices of the housing professional. It became evident to me as I journeyed from practice to academic research on practice, that one's perspective shifts as one's relation to the object of attention changes. It also became evident that practice, viewed from one perspective, can appear as 'cruel', 'heartless', even 'barbaric', yet be deemed perfectly 'rational' and 'normal' from another standpoint. My research has made me realise that housing professionals who preside over evictions are not monsters; rather, housing professionals, like everyone else, want a fair and just world. Indeed, they want to be at the very heart of safe communities where people can thrive. But they are constrained by the political structures that have a significant influence on their practice. The rightward tilting of the bureaucratic state involves the constant encroachment of the surveillance and disciplinary arm of the state into a system of welfare provision that already had a social control function, extends the punitive obsession with social tenants and those at the margins such as undocumented migrants, and people seeking asylum. This distorts the notion of the Civic state, and thus alters the way people imagine and utilise the Civic polity. Regulatory capitalism continually expands, redrawing the boundaries of its own jurisdiction to encompass more and more of the field of social welfare. The regulatory oversight of the inspection and audit culture in the welfare service sector compels social landlords to behave like private sector entities, adopting a business approach to delivery that privileges neoliberal forms of managerialism over traditional tenant-lead practices that are founded on community values (Jacobs, 2019, Jacobs and Manzi, 2000, 2019a, and 2019b).

If human 'emotions' and 'instinctual gut-feelings' have a political structure, then it can be said that changes in the political economy, such as a rightward tilting or leftward tilting, will have the latent potential to reconfigure the things we 'care' about, the things we see as being 'fair' or those things that deserve our new sense of 'loyalty' and protection from 'harm'. It is this paradigm shift in how economies are run and political systems govern that offers the greatest potential for significant changes in the way we live and work. There is no doubt that new parallax gaps will open up between the newly defined and reconstituted institutions, organisations and groups charged with the task of taking the lead in our de-carbonised, de-growth, ecologically friendly, green new future. The real sea change that could emerge from the redistribution of riches that will accompany hyper automation, is the potential to abolish, not only the wage relation, but to abolish the rent relation altogether. This is one of the most radical opportunities that could be realised in a new economy. One such organisation to embrace the need for this green new future and the opportunities it brings is Commonweal, a 'Think and Do Tank', based in Scotland. Having recently published its own comprehensive Green New Deal entitled 'Our Common Home', it states that;

> Our era is an era of crisis – economic crisis, social crisis, environmental crisis. From climate change to ever-widening inequality, people fear that we may be condemned to a future worse than our present. People look forward with fear, they long for a plan which persuades them the future can be better than our present. This is that plan, the Common Home Plan.
> (Commonweal 2019: 7)

With ambitions that match those of the great infrastructure projects of the Victorians, this plan does not shy away from the fact that change of a paradigmatic nature is required. It acknowledges that the kinds of solutions necessary to undo the decades of social, economic and environmental harm require interventions of the proportions not seen since the founding of the NHS and the welfare state. On the issue of housing, Commonweal envisage a green new future, based around communities and sustainable local economies:

> Scotland needs to radically transform the housing sector. From building energy efficient houses fit for the 21st century, through building communities rather than dormitories, to changing the way we rent and own property to avoid being exploited by private developers and landlords, Scotland has the opportunity to be truly transformative in a way that directly impacts the way that people live.

Chapter 3 looked at the relationship between the dominant tenure and the dominant means of wealth accumulation and surplus value extraction that it served. The suggestion was made that in just over 100 years, we have come full circle, with the return of the private rented market and its corresponding economic form, rentier capitalism. If the private housing revolution resulted in much better conditions and security of tenure on its return in 21st century, then the forthcoming revolution that will bring us back to some form of universal social housing has every chance of being a much improved system, having learned from the design mistakes and planning disasters of the first great social housing experiment. Such a paradigm shift also has the potential to restore communities, addressing the mental health crisis and the suicide epidemic that is killing increasing numbers of young people in the UK. UBS and the inclusion of housing will not only end evictions for rent arrears, it will provide the opportunity to rebuild communities and to live in well designed, practical and sustainable neighbourhoods, that will be necessary for people to work together and take responsibility for the creation of a sustainable future.

From a political-realist perspective, the impediment to such paradigmatic change is not lack of ambition, nor is it a deficiency in knowledge or understanding. What will stand in the way of a green new future for housing and indeed the wider transformation that will facilitate such change, are the forces that currently dominate the political economy. Just as multinational carbon polluters spend sizable chunks of their profits trying to convince sections of the population that climate change has nothing to do with carbon emissions, so too will global corporations who profit from rent and financial speculation robustly resist the implementation of UBS. Politics is the process through which individuals and groups seek to either conserve the structures of the world or transform them. In the past, such battles have been waged between those who occupy favourable positions in social space (those who are least likely to be advocates of change) and those who occupy dominated positions (those for whom change would be of most benefit). This future battle will undoubtedly take place between those on the side of capital and those on the side of the planet. There really can only be one winner, since failure to act now may create more wealth for some in the short term, but no one will be around long enough to see them enjoy it.

Recapitulation

In developing a relational model to understanding practice, this book has taken the interview data from three case studies relating to evictions, and by adding layers of analysis, built up a more nuanced understanding of evictions in the UK. This relational approach to understanding practice has emphasised the extent to which power, housing and politics are not only interconnected, they are inextricably linked. Several insights emerged from these analyses. People are in the world, but the world is also in them, a fact that gives weight to the contention that agency is, to a certain extent, structured. The divisions that arise from the subjective and objective worlds, although false binaries constructed by our diacritical minds, are nonetheless real, since human beings perceive them as such. The best way to understand practice is, therefore, to look at not one or the other, but the relation between the two. This can be observed as the interaction between people and the worlds they inhabit, a relation from which practices arise and form collective conventions and knowledges. Although people make the world that makes them, the world is privileged in that its effects on individuals tend to be far greater than the effects individuals can have on the world. This exposes the political nature of professional practice. When the denial of 'interest' is masked under the cloak of 'disinterestedness', and the 'arbitrary' and 'contingent' structures of the social world are 'misrecognised' as being 'natural' and 'necessary', then the highly political nature of power relations become hidden behind the innocent mask of social relations. Ultimately, these insights render the common-sense liberal approach to housing studies, of little value since they capture only the superficial nature of reality. Rather than exposing and challenging the operation of power and domination, the liberal, common sense view enforces it. This makes it a wonderful means by which to obtain favour with the funding bodies of the state, and to build relationships with the state's institutions in the name of collaboration, but is useless for understanding the world or for holding power to account. As Hegel says, the appearance of things and their essence rarely coincide, as I found out on my own journey from practice to academia, when I realised that I had been incorporated into the very system I thought I was fighting. Critical reason is essential, lest social science, and social scientists, be unwittingly used in the service of powerful interests.

As for those who may be involved in evictions or the task of trying to prevent them, until the choice between capitalism and planet is taken seriously enough to instigate the necessary paradigm shift to herald the green new housing deal, we are going to have to do the best with what we have. Hopefully this book can make us think about some of the things that previously escaped our conscious awareness. Hopefully we can all become more aware of the 'hidden aspects' of our professional practice. Perhaps even see through the political veil that masks the 'arbitrary' and make us question what we perceive to be 'necessary'. Once we move beyond the limits imposed on our understanding by binary thinking, and once we move beyond the petty squabbles that arise from our parallax differences, we can work towards the promotion of a paradigm shift so significant that it will have the power to transform so much more than just our housing system. If we are to forge ahead and create a green new future, then 'rent free', well-designed housing in communities where people want to live, is quite possibly the very best starting point.

References

Bastani A. (2019) *Fully Automated Luxury Communism: A Manifesto*, Verso: London.

Bourdieu P. (1977) *Outline of a Theory of Practice*, [R. Nice, transl], vol. 16, Cambridge: Cambridge University Press.

Bourdieu P. (1990) *The Logic of Practice*, Cambridge: Polity Press.

Bourdieu P. (2000) *Pascallian Meditations*, London: Polity Press.

Fisher M. (2009) *Capitalist Realism: Is There No Alternative*, London: Zero Books.

Jacobs K. (2019) *Neoliberal Housing Policy: An International Perspective*, New York: Routledge.

Jacobs K. and Manzi T. (2000) 'Performance indicators and social constructivism: conflict and control in housing management'. *Critical Social Policy*, 20 (1): 85–103.

Jacobs K. and Manzi T. (2019a) 'Conceptualising "financialisation": governance, organisational behaviour and social interaction in UK housing'. *International Journal of Housing Policy*. DOI: 10.1080/19491247.2018.1540737.

Jacobs K. and Manzi T. (2019b) 'Neoliberalism as entrepreneurial governmentality: contradictions and dissonance within contemporary English housing associations'. *Housing Studies*. https://doi.org/10.1080/02673037.2019.1617411.

Index

For Product Safety Concerns and Information please contact our EU representative GPSR@taylorandfrancis.com
Taylor & Francis Verlag GmbH, Kaufingerstraße 24, 80331 München, Germany

www.ingramcontent.com/pod-product-compliance
Ingram Content Group UK Ltd.
Pitfield, Milton Keynes, MK11 3LW, UK
UKHW022124190926
475702UK00013B/1624
9780367419684